100 years of the
FORTH BRIDGE

Edited by Roland Paxton

Thomas Telford, London

Published by Thomas Telford Ltd, Thomas Telford House, 1 Heron Quay, London E14 9XF

First published 1990

Conversion factors

1 inch	2·54 cm
1 foot	30·48 cm
1 yard	91·44 cm
1 mile	1·61 km
1 mph	1·61 km/h
1 ton/in^2	15·44 MPa
1 lb/ft^2	0·05 kN/m^2
1 hp	$2·7 \times 10^3$ kJ/h

A CIP catalogue record for this book is available from the British Library

ISBN 0 7277 1600 X

Typeset by Pentacor PLC, High Wycombe, Bucks
Printed and bound in Great Britain by Redwood Press Limited, Melksham, Wilts

Introductory message from ScotRail

Richard Spoors, *Civil Engineer, ScotRail*

During construction work visitors from far and wide made their way to the Firth of Forth to witness the vast amounts of steel, stone and concrete take shape to form the Forth Bridge—the pinnacle of the technology of the day and one of the world's most instantly recognisable structures.

The purpose of this bridge was to allow trains to cross from one side of the Firth to the other and gain better access to the north of Scotland. That function is still being fulfilled with some 200 trains a day crossing over it.

In this centenary year of the opening of the Forth Bridge many thousands of words and photographs have been produced about the world famous bridge. However, this publication—written by engineers and containing much that is new and thought-provoking—is particularly appropriate. The building of the Forth Bridge was a great engineering feat; it has been maintained by civil engineers, and it is civil engineers who will maintain it for the next 100 years.

Maintaining the safety and integrity of the Forth Bridge is an onerous responsibility which the railway civil engineer in Scotland carries out with traditional expertise.

Richard Spoors.

Foreword

The Earl of Elgin and Kincardine

One of the oldest fascinations of life, especially as darkness falls of an evening, is to listen to a good story. This series of talks was aimed as the starting power for the centenary celebrations of the Forth Bridge; but, as talk followed talk, more and more wonder and amazement were engendered. There is no doubt whatever that, while every aspect of bridge building and maintenance was uncovered, a most deeply held interest was also discovered in one of the greatest structures produced by man's hands.

Those of us who listened were almost made aghast at the sheer confidence with which the work was progressed. We were touched, too, to feel that although the bridge was built for the age of steam, many of the men most adept at the building had learned their agility in the hardest of ways—upon the tall masts of sailing ships. There were times when we looked at the structure, bristling with cranes and hoists and men, and wondered how such a conglomeration could achieve such perfection: but it did, and in these various chapters the reader will find a sumptuous story, with determination to overcome all odds beaming from both the obvious and the most curious of circumstances.

I am greatly indebted to Roland Paxton of the Institution of Civil Engineers for his persistence in persuasion which has linked so many eminent people to tell so great a story.

Preface

As their contribution to the centenary of the Forth Bridge, the Institution of Civil Engineers and the National Museums of Scotland decided to hold a series of public lectures about the bridge from the standpoint of present engineering knowledge. What could be more appropriate than knowledgeable engineers paying tribute to their distinguished predecessors? Coverage would include earlier Forth crossing projects, the design, construction and maintenance of the bridge, the men responsible for it and a foray into the future. After much thought and activity six lectures were arranged. They were read at the Royal Museum of Scotland in Edinburgh on six Tuesday evenings from 27 February to 3 April 1990. Attendances were of the order of 240–300 and the lectures were very well received. With this encouragement it was decided to test public support for their possible publication from the audience at the last two lectures. An announcement was made and within a week or so 240 people had indicated their willingness to subscribe for a copy. It was decided to go ahead with a view to publication before the main centenary celebrations in October.

The brief for each lecture was carefully defined to minimise duplication and, although some minor editorial discretion in this respect has been exercised on scripts, it was felt nevertheless that the published versions should substantially represent the content of the presentations as delivered. The extent of any artist's licence away from the titles is left for the reader to judge! Obtaining scripts from busy professional men against a tight time-scale is not the easiest of tasks and in these circumstances differences of style have been considered acceptable. The lectures were profusely illustrated by slides of considerable range and impact. Over 130 of these illustrations are included in the book.

As another contribution to the centenary, the organisers held a schools' competition throughout Scotland on the same theme as the last lecture: 'Crossing the Forth in 2090'. It too was successful. This is an appropriate opportunity to thank again Professor Paul Jowitt of Heriot-Watt University and Jack Christie of Moray House College for their diligent and, at times, daunting adjudication of over 200, many multifaceted, entries in four age bands. Also, Brian Speedie, Museum Education Officer, is thanked for his excellent administration which involved contact with nearly 4000 schools. The entries would have made a fascinating book in themselves. In this volume the opportunity is taken to include the details of the most outstanding entry as a tribute to the bridge from the schools of Scotland.

Such a publishing venture as this is not achieved without a great deal of effort from many people. Much of this has already been acknowledged in individual contributions but even so, thank you all. In particular, the Hon. Sir William McAlpine, a most memorable chairman of 'Maintaining the bridge' and Leslie Soane collectively with Lord Elgin played a crucial catalytic role in getting this publication to the slipway. It would not have been launched without essential sponsorship from ScotRail, the Forth Bridge Centenary Trust, Thomas Telford Ltd and the Institution of Civil Engineers. The generosity of the sponsors has resulted in a high quality book at a reasonable price and it is recorded here with gratitude. In connection with the Institution's contribution, particular thanks are due to President Peter Stott, John C. McKenzie and W. D. Cormie of the secretariat and to Past Presidents Dr W. G. N. Geddes and A. C. Paterson and the Local Association Chairman Douglas Gallacher for so ably chairing lectures. Lord Elgin's characteristically stylish launch of the series and his active interest throughout was very much appreciated, as was Murray Grigor's closing chairmanship with its schools' prize-giving and bonus of a video-showing of his magnificent multi-projector slide presentation about the bridge.

In conclusion, many thanks for their willing co-operation and support are also due to the Institution's partner in this enterprise, the National Museums of Scotland through Dr Robert Anderson, Director, Dr S. Brock, D. Bryden and other members of the Museum's staff. Also thanked are: members of the committee of the Edinburgh and East of Scotland Association of the Institution, particularly, in addition to its above-mentioned chairman, Colin Beak, Secretary and Alan Woodhead, Treasurer; members of the Institution's Panel for Historical Engineering Works, particularly Michael Chrimes of its secretariat, Mrs Sandra Purves, Scottish Group Secretary, and Ronald Birse for indispensable help in organising the competition and for video-recording Professor Happold's lecture. Last, but not least, I wish to thank my co-authors for their masterly contributions and their forbearance at editorial intrusions into their busy lives. It is hoped that they and the reader will consider this contribution to the annals of the great bridge to have been worthwhile.

Roland A. Paxton
July 1990

Contents

Chapter 1.   Engineering challenges before the bridge.   *R. A. Paxton*   1

Chapter 2.   Design of the bridge.   *J. S. Shipway*   36

Chapter 3.   Construction of the bridge.   *W. R. Cox*   67

Chapter 4.   Maintaining the bridge.   *D. Grant*   91

Chapter 5.   The men behind the bridge.   *R. M. Birse*   109

Chapter 6.   Crossing the Forth in 2090.   *E. Happold*   143

Result of Scottish Schools' Forth Bridge Competition   162

Index   164

CHAPTER 1

Engineering challenges before the bridge

R. A. Paxton, *Chairman, ICE Panel for Historical Engineering Works*

This Chapter identifies and assesses engineering challenges associated with crossing the Forth at or near Queensferry from *c*. 208 to 1873, with reference to the practice of various civil engineers in the work contexts of harbours and ferries, tunnels, and road and railway schemes. Particular consideration is devoted to the improvement of ferry landings by Smeaton, Rennie, Stevenson and Telford; impracticable proposals for tunnels and bridges; and the railway triple challenge of Sir Thomas Bouch, including his questionable Charlestown Bridge design of 1865. Aspects of the evolution of structural practice are cited, but the Chapter essentially outlines the early history of the Queensferry crossing from an engineering standpoint. Its purpose is to serve as an introduction to the magnificent achievement of the Forth Bridge, one of the great feats of civilisation.

Harbour and ferry improvements

A regular ferry service is known to have operated across the Forth at Queensferry as early as the 12th century, using natural rock landings including 'The Binks', immediately west of Queensferry harbour (Fig. 1.1). It is not certain when the first artificial landings were constructed, but by 1710 small structures existed at the Hawes Pier, Queensferry Harbour (partly founded on a rock outcrop), and at North Queensferry.

In 1760, although the Queensferry 'passage ferry' was the most frequented in Scotland, the poor condition of the loading and landing places, especially at low water, was 'not only highly disagreeable and inexpeditious, but even dangerous'.[1] As the communications improvements associated with the Industrial Revolution began to gather pace nationally, it became essential to improve the ferry. In 1772 a petition was sent to the Forfeited Estates Commissioners from Fife JPs and the ferry owners requesting financial aid towards a £980 package of improvements.[2] The name of the engineer, if any, who made these proposals has not been found. The Commissioners consulted John Smeaton (1724–92) (Fig. 1.2), 'the father of civil engineering', who was already making an important contribution to the Scottish infrastructure. In addition to engineering the Forth and Clyde Canal, he had introduced major improvements to the machinery at Carron Ironworks and built large bridges at Perth and Coldstream.[3] He had also reported on numerous harbours.

Smeaton's report on the Queensferry landings (1772)[4]
Smeaton considered the principal defect of the ferry to be in its landing places, which being 'in a great measure furnished by nature . . . require a little assistance from art'. He drew particular attention to the lack of low-water landings, by which 'travellers are often detained when the wind is fair and afterwards further detained by the winds coming foul'. Then, as now, the prevailing wind was from the west and there were strong cross-currents.

Smeaton recommended a spread of landings on each shore to enable boats to cross more frequently without tacking, thus saving time. More particularly, his recommendations included improving a 96 yard length of the Grey Landing (near Queensferry Harbour) down to low water, to face both east and west. At the West Hall (Hawes) Pier he proposed part facing, part building on and part levelling the rock for 142 yards down to a point 5–6 ft above the sand. On the north shore he advocated the extension of Craig End

Fig. 1.1. The Queensferry Shore rock landings from Hawes Pier via 'The Craigs' to 'The Binks'

Fig. 1.2. (far left) John Smeaton FRS

Fig. 1.3. (left) John Rennie FRS (after Behnes)

Pier (the town pier) by 53 yards and the improvement of East Ness Landing access by providing a smooth road across the rough rocks. This work was to be done by blasting or by bolting timber to the rock, to take the wheels of carriages in the manner of a railroad.[5] It would appear that Smeaton's advice, or much of it, was heeded by the applicants and grant-aiding authorities, as by July 1777 the Royal Burghs of Scotland had contributed £300[1] and the Forfeited Estates Commissioners £600; the latter on the basis of the ferry forming part of a military road and being the most frequented sea passage in Scotland.[2] In 1775, the Trustees for the Improvement of Fisheries and Manufactures also contributed to the repair of Newhalls Pier and a landing east of North Ferry.[6]

Baird's report on the improvement of Queensferry Harbour (1817)
In the latter part of the 18th century, Queensferry Harbour comprised a pair of not quite parallel piers curving inward at their seaward ends to form an entrance from the north, with a ferry landing place on the outside of the east pier. The harbour was improved to a design of 1817 by Hugh Baird (1770–1827), engineer to the Union Canal, who advised turning the west pier at a right angle and running it eastward to a new entrance in the north-east corner of the harbour. This work, which entailed rebuilding the head of the east pier adjoining the ferry landing, was carried out; thus the harbour was brought more or less to its present form.[7]

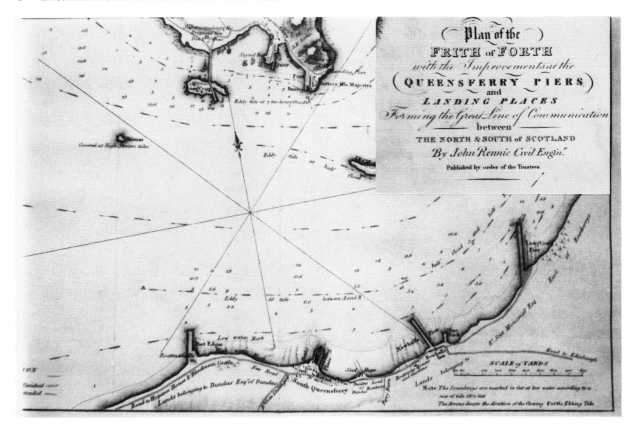

Fig. 1.4. Queensferry pier and landing improvements: Rennie 1809–17

Major improvements to the ferry 1808–17

The ferry improvements completed in *c.* 1777, which presumably resulted in two good landings on each shore, sufficed for over two decades, but with increased trade, commerce and travel a better crossing facility became necessary. In May 1809 an Act[8] was passed vesting the ferry in new Trustees as part of the improvement of the Great North Road from Edinburgh to Perth and beyond, and major development ensued. With a net capital of £18 500 after paying off the former owners, the Trustees set to work on improving the whole establishment to the plans of the eminent engineer John Rennie (1761–1821) (Figs 1.3 and 1.4). His recent work in the locality had included the construction of Musselburgh Bridge, Bell Rock Lighthouse, Leith, Berwick and St Andrews harbours; recommending improvements at Newhaven, Charlestown, Burntisland and Perth harbours; and proposing the Berwick to Kelso railway and multispan cast iron arch bridge over the Forth at Alloa.[9]

Rennie developed Smeaton's recommendation to establish a spread of landings on each shore, thus enabling boats to cross the river diagonally with assistance from wind and tide without having to tack. By 1812 Newhalls

(Hawes) Pier had been enlarged to a length of about 240 yards (scaled) and rebuilt to its present form with a central breakwater flanked by paved roads at a total cost of £8696. A new pier about 200 yards long had been built at Port Edgar for £4763[6] and a small pier at Portnuick for use by cattle, involving rockblasting to provide sufficient water depth. On the north shore a landing place and approach road had been constructed at the west side of the Battery, also a new house for the ferry superintendent and a signal house with accommodation for a boat's crew below. On the south shore new buildings included a boatman's house at Port Edgar, six boatman's houses at Newhalls, and probably the small lighthouse at Newhalls Pier. The improvements on the south side fulfilled their purpose of encouraging the keeping of some boats there overnight. Previously the general custom had been to berth boats at night on the north shore only which often caused delay to travellers from the South. These works were executed with the solidity and excellence that characterised Rennie's practice, and most of them still exist. Unfortunately, their cost, which included some unforeseen extra work, considerably exceeded the initial capital, almost £34 000 having been spent with two piers still not constructed. To give an idea of the scale of use of the improvements engineered by Rennie, in the year ending 15 May 1811, 83 220 persons, 5769

Fig. 1.5. Longcraig Pier 1990: Rennie; constructed 1816–17

carriages and carts, 44 365 horses, cattle and sheep, and 5520 barrels crossed by the ferry.[10] (In 1989 about 30 million persons crossed by road and 3 million by rail!)

A new act[11] was invoked in July 1814 authorising expenditure of a further £20 000 to construct Longcraig Pier on the south shore and Longcraig Island Pier on the north. The site of Longcraig Pier was advertised to be determined on 13 May 1816,[12] and by October 1817 the work to Rennie's plan was almost completed (Fig. 1.5)[13] The completion date of 1812 given by Graham[7] is, uncharacteristically, incorrect—Longcraig Island Pier was not built, but a pier close by to the east was constructed later.

Another engineer, Robert Stevenson (1772–1850) (Fig. 1.6), constructor of the Bell Rock Lighthouse was called in by the ferry superintendent in 1817 to advise on lighting arrangements. He recommended repositioning the signal house reflector at the pier head at 12–15 ft above high water level, presumably creating the small hexagonal tower lighthouse that still exists. The reflector would probably have been of the parabolic type of 21–24 inches diameter, and the light source an Argand oil lamp, the whole apparatus producing a light intensity of the order of 2000–3000 candle power.

Just when costly near-perfection had been achieved at this *ne plus ultra* of sailing establishments, the enterprise encountered major competition from steamboats which, not being so dependent on wind and tide, were quicker in operation. These started operation on the Fife and Midlothian or 'Broad Ferry' between Newhaven and Dysart in September 1819. By the autumn of 1820, the Fife and Midlothian Ferry was operating three steamboats from Newhaven, resulting in the Queensferry Passage losing about two-thirds of its coach passenger traffic.[14] Difficult tidal conditions and the design of and spread of the piers were not conducive to the general introduction of steamboats on the Queensferry Passage. Its Trustees, after considering various types of paddle steamer, probably including Stevenson's novel 'Dalswinton' internal paddle steamboat which he advocated for use on this ferry,[15] commissioned a paddle steamboat to the design of their superintendent. The vessel, named the 'Queen Margaret', entered service in October 1821, towing large and small sailing boats in its wake. On the south side at low water only Longcraig Pier had sufficient water depth to accommodate the boat, and because of the incompatibility of its external side paddles with the pier profile wheeled traffic could not be handled. In 1821 a fleet of sailing boats was introduced, but the whole operation, although well managed, failed to meet the increasing steamboat challenge from the 'Broad Ferry' and in 1828 the Trustees consulted Britain's leading civil engineer, Thomas Telford (1757–1834) (Fig. 1.7), with a view to improving the situation.

Telford's reports on the Forth Ferries (1828)
Telford reported that the probable future revenue of the ferry was incompat-

Fig. 1.6. (far left) Robert Stevenson FRSE

Fig. 1.7. (left) Thomas Telford FRS (after S. Lane)

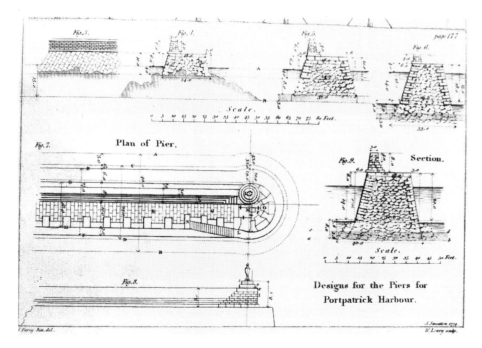

Fig. 1.8. Typical harbour construction: Smeaton 1770–72

Fig. 1.9. Horse-whim and machinery to mine-shaft chain: Agricola 1556

ible with changing the whole mode of operation from a sailing to a steamboat system. He advised adopting only improvements which could be accomplished at a justifiable expense, adding 'That such are become indispensably necessary the rapid improvement of conveyance on all sides is sufficient evidence'.[16] Telford's recommendations included an extension of the Signal House (Craig End) Pier into deeper water, a measure intended to provide a safer wharfage on its eastern side, to protect the extremity of the Battery Pier, and to supply additional accommodation. He commented that to have extended this pier before the introduction of steamboats would have obstructed the necessary tacks for sailing boats making passage to the south. On the south side Telford considered it impracticable to obtain a greater low-water depth at Newhall Pier without unwarrantable expense. For low-water use he recommended Longcraig Pier, where the water depth was already sufficient, but because this pier was exposed to the prevalent westerly winds and the force of the ebbing tide current, he advised provision of a rubble stone breakwater alongside it at a short distance to the west. Telford left the question of the detail and estimates for these improvements to his Edinburgh civil engineering associate James Jardine (1776–1858). From a comparison of Rennie's plan and the 1856 Ordnance Survey map, Signal House pier appears to have subsequently been extended. Longcraig breakwater was not built.

In 1828 Telford was also consulted by the Fife and Midlothian Lower Ferry owners, with a very different outcome. He considered its revenue prospects to support almost £61 000 worth of improvements, including a new pier at Burntisland and a new landing at Newhaven 400 yards beyond the end of the existing pier end so as to achieve a 10 ft lowwater depth for steamboats.[3] This work was not carried out, but major ferry developments eventually ensued at Granton and Burntisland.

Development of engineering practice 1770–1830
In structural engineering terms the works referred to above would have required little in the way of strength calculations, mainly consisting of foundations, gravity masonry walls and timber piles and beams in foundations, and timber and cast iron as struts and tension members. Practices adopted were based on experience or experiment. Piers generally consisted of a pair of masonry walls separated by uncoursed stone hearting (Figs 1.5 and 1.8).

From *c.* 1800, cast iron beams, columns, plates and other castings were available. Wrought iron was obtainable up to about 3 inch diameter cross-section in long lengths and as narrow plates. From *c.* 1800 portable steam-engines were used increasingly for powering pumps, dredgers and other equipment. By 1830, the use of artificial cement, mass concrete in foundations and more effectively preserved timber was developing. The use of steel and reinforced concrete in structures did not begin until the latter part of the

Fig. 1.10. Forth tunnel: Grieve's proposed cross-section, 1806

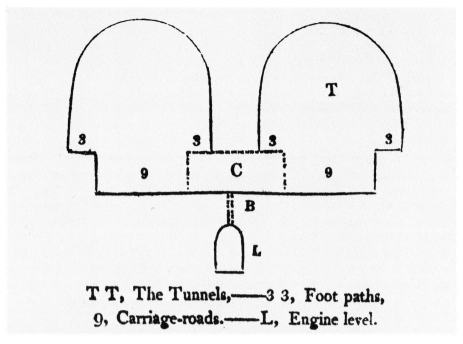

T T, The Tunnels,——3 3, Foot paths,
9, Carriage-roads.——L, Engine level.

century. 'Strength of materials' education for engineers from textbooks, as distinct from 'word of mouth' and experience, was in its infancy; it gathered momentum from *c.* 1817, developing rapidly in the 1820s mainly on a practical and empirical basis. From 1822, Tredgold's textbook on cast iron[18] with its empirically derived safe load tables was useful to engineers in designing beams of up to 30 ft span and columns up to 24 ft high. The foundation in 1818 of the Institution of Civil Engineers as a forum for the exchange of knowledge represented a landmark in the development of engineering education. The reliable theoretical approach to engineering design now practised universally had not evolved to any extent by 1830.

Tunnel projects

Tunnels under the Forth existed at least four centuries ago (Fig. 1.9). In 1618, John Taylor ('The Water Poet') wrote of Sir George Bruce of Carnock's 'moat' coal-pit at Culross with its sea cofferdam entrance

'I went in by sea, and out by land' (this being possible because) 'at low water, the sea being ebd away, and a great part of the sand bare; upon this same sand (being mixed with rockes and cragges) did the master of this great worke build a round circular frame of stone, very thicke, strong, and joined together with glutinous or bituminous matter so high withall that the sea at the greates flood . . . can neither dissolve the stones . . . or yet overflow the height of it. Within this round frame . . . hee did set workmen to digge with mattockes, pickaxes . . . They did dig forty feet downe right into . . . that which they expected, which was sea-cole . . . they following the veine of the mine did dig forward still: So that in the space of eight and twenty or nine and twenty yeeres, they have digged more than an English mile under the sea . . . the mine is most artificially cut like an arch or vault . . . that a man may walk upright in most places . . . The sea at certaines places doth leake . . . into the mine . . . is all conveyed to one well neere the land; where . . . a device like a horse-mill, that with three horses and a great chain of iron going downeward many fathoms, with thirty-six buckets fastened to the chaine, of which eighteene goe down still to be filled, and eighteene ascend up . . . which doe emptie themselves (without any mans labour) into a trough that conveyes the water into the sea againe . . .'[19] (Fig. 1.9)

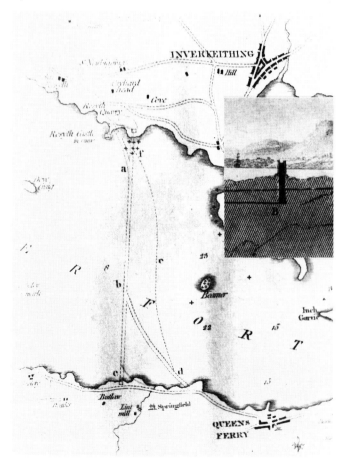

Fig. 1.11. Forth tunnel plan, 1806: (inset) moated shaft, looking west

The works described are of outstanding significance in Scotland's industrial history, and provide an insight into the entrepreneurial enterprise of Sir George Bruce, gentleman coal-owner who can be considered a civil engineer in all but name. (Smeaton is believed to have been the first to call himself 'civil engineer' nearly two centuries later.) When leasing the mine at Culross in 1575, Bruce's 'great knowledge and skill in machinery' was acknowledged, and he was thought the most suitable person to re-open the then abandoned mine.[20] He adopted the best continental 'state of the art' practice of Georg Agricola and others.[21] By 1595 Bruce had constructed a storage reservoir on Culross Muir to guarantee water supply to a colliery water-mill at or near the horse-gin site. He also erected a windmill and a tide-mill as alternative power sources.[22] The workings are believed to have extended some two miles under the sea before the mine was flooded over the cofferdam in a storm in 1625.[23]

Fig. 1.12. View along the proposed tunnel line from near its north end, c. 1890

It has been written that a proposal for a tunnel under the Forth at Inchgarvie was mooted about 1790,[24] but this does not seem to have been taken seriously, possibly because of the impracticability of mining through

whinstone. Fifteen years later a proposal for a tunnel 1½ miles to the west received wide consideration.[25] The engineering case for it was supported by successful under-sea tunnelling precedents at the Culross, Bo'ness and Whitehaven coal mines, and operational canal tunnels at Harecastle and Sapperton. By 1805, the Bo'ness workings had extended about a mile under the Forth at depths of 20–80 fathoms*. The Valleyfield under-sea workings of Sir Robert Preston at Culross were so dry that they could be drained 'by a boy with a bucket'.[27] At Whitehaven the workings were at a depth of 80–150 fathoms under the sea, with access via white-walled tunnels on a 1 in 6 gradient.

Forth tunnel proposals 1805–7
In November 1805 a William Vazie, probably with a mining background, sought the opinion of a leading Edinburgh mining engineer, John Grieve, as to whether a tunnel under the Forth from Rosyth Castle to the opposite shore was practicable. Grieve thought that it was, as the rock was likely to be passable freestone, but called for this to be confirmed by borings all along the tunnel line. On the basis of a maximum water depth of 11 fathoms from a chart, Grieve suggested a maximum depth for the tunnel sole of 30 fathoms. He proposed twin 15 ft wide arched tunnels with a central drain level beneath (Fig. 1.10). The tunnels were to have had 500 yard entry sections parallel to each shore with gradients of 1 in 25 so as to achieve 50 ft of cover before turning under the sea. From these turnings the main tunnels would have descended for 1800 yards from each side at a gradient of 1 in 45, meeting midway at the maximum depth. For drainage Grieve proposed constructing two moated engine pits over 200 ft deep at each low-water mark. At the bottom of the pits steam-engines and pumps were to have been installed. Grieve estimated the cost of the tunnel at £160 000–170 000, with a 4 year construction period.

In the summer of 1806 Vazie and his associate Taylor, probably James Taylor (1753–1825), mining agent, reported in similar vein after a site visit with Grieve. Some alterations were suggested to meet objections from the Earl of Hopetoun. The proposed tunnel entrance to the south was moved westward to within a few hundred yards of Queensferry (Fig. 1.11). To obviate smoke nuisance from the steam-engine and to reduce activity near the grounds of Hopetoun House, it was proposed that any buildings associated with the project, including the permanent steam pumping installation, would be located on the north shore. A busy little town was envisaged at Rosyth 'with the Castle in its bosom' (Fig. 1.12). Alternative cross-sections were given, both with separate carriageways for 'comers' and 'goers'. More thought had been given to passing under the deep part of the river:

---

*1 fathom = 6 feet

'If the boring should in any manner of way leave the investigation incomplete . . . it may become necessary to advance . . . with caution . . . by putting down pits at low water mark . . . to the necessary depth and cutting a communication by a level between them . . . Such a level will at all events be necessary as a drain . . . for drawing the water from the tunnel . . . Will require to have placed . . . the engines necessary for the great work . . . no new or additional expense . . . an expenditure would be incurred, including engines, from 12 to 15000 £ . . .'[25]

The proposal was also supported by the civil engineer Robert Bald (c. 1778–1861), who advised making soundings and borings as a preparatory step. The Scots Magazine was 'happy to see that this undertaking is in a great state of forwardness and that a number of noblemen and gentlemen of the first respectability have organised themselves into a regular body for the purpose of carrying it into effect'.[26] In March 1807 a Dr Millar and Vazie republished an enlarged illustrated edition of the various reports with an economic case.[27] The tunnel was not started, probably more for economic reasons than doubts about its engineering practicability.

Assessment
It was fortunate for the promoters that the project did not proceed, as the ground under the deep part of the river would have proved very different to

Fig. 1.13. View of preglacial Forth Valley at Queensferry, Cadell 1913: NB the approximate tunnel line has been added by the Author

Fig. 1.14. Possible Roman campaign boat bridge, Queensferry, c. 208: drawn by D. Cameron with advice on detail from Dr G. Maxwell and the Author

that imagined. The mining experts of the day expected the freestone to extend from shore to shore, a concept proved as late as 1964 several miles west when the Kinneil and Valleyfield mines were joined, *but at a depth of about 1800 ft.*[28] At the depth of 180 ft proposed for the Queensferry Tunnel, the miners would have encountered a deep channel in the bed of the river filled with sand and silt. The Scottish geologist H. M. Cadell of Grange drew attention to this subject in 1913,[23] and provided a dramatic sketch of his impression of the preglacial Forth valley, complete with mammoth and Forth Bridge (Fig. 1.13). Although Cadell's concept of deeply buried preglacial river channels is no longer considered tenable,[29] there is no doubt that a channel containing a considerable depth of sand and silt does exist, whatever its origin, and his sketch serves to illustrate the difficulty the tunnellers would have had to confront. The question now is whether the tunnel could have been constructed in such material in 1807. A review of contemporary experience indicates the answer.

From 1796–98 an engineer, Ralph Dodd, proposed a tunnel under the Tyne between North and South Shields.[30] Although this tunnel did not proceed, it was the precursor of his ambitious scheme for a 16 ft diameter road tunnel under the Thames from Gravesend to Tilbury, which actually started.[31] Difficulties with groundwater in the preparatory operation of sinking a shaft for this tunnel in sandy material proved so great that the entire capital for the project was consumed without even achieving the shaft, and the project was abandoned in 1803. Undaunted by this setback, a Cornish mining engineer, Robert Vazie, known as 'The Mole' (he may have been related to William Vazie) commenced work on the Thames Archway tunnel at Limehouse in

1805, where he was employed until his dismissal in October 1807. Difficulties in sinking a 13 ft diameter shaft through gravel and quicksand again proved so great that operations were suspended. Rennie and another leading engineer, William Chapman, were consulted but could not agree on a course of action. Work eventually recommenced under the direction of Richard Trevithick, a notable Cornish mining engineer (and 'father of the locomotive'), on a 5 ft pilot driftway ultimately intended to form a drain under the tunnel. A 30 hp steam engine was used to pump out water. Good progress was made until, nearing the far side of the river, sand and water frequently burst into the driftway, and work stopped in 1808. In March 1809 a premium was offered to any person furnishing a plan enabling the tunnel to be completed. At least 53 plans were received and examined by the eminent

Fig. 1.15. Ironmaking c. 1850: rolling mill, blast and puddling

engineers Dr Charles Hutton and William Jessop, who, after due consideration, concluded that 'an underground tunnel which would be useful to the public and beneficial to the adventurers is impracticable'. The problem had confounded the experts. Many thousands of pounds had been irretrievably lost and not a single brick of the tunnel had been laid.[32–34]

There can be no doubt that the proposed Forth Tunnel, involving a substantial length of construction in river-bed silt and sand, was beyond the means at the command of its engineers. A considerably deeper tunnel with the same gradients and passing under the soft material would have been ruled out on grounds of cost—it would, however, be an option to consider for a new crossing of the Forth today.

Fig. 1.16. Proposed 'chain' bridge at Queensferry, Anderson 1818: note the stay design and the ironwork stretching machine; the inset and cross-section relate to the catenary cable design

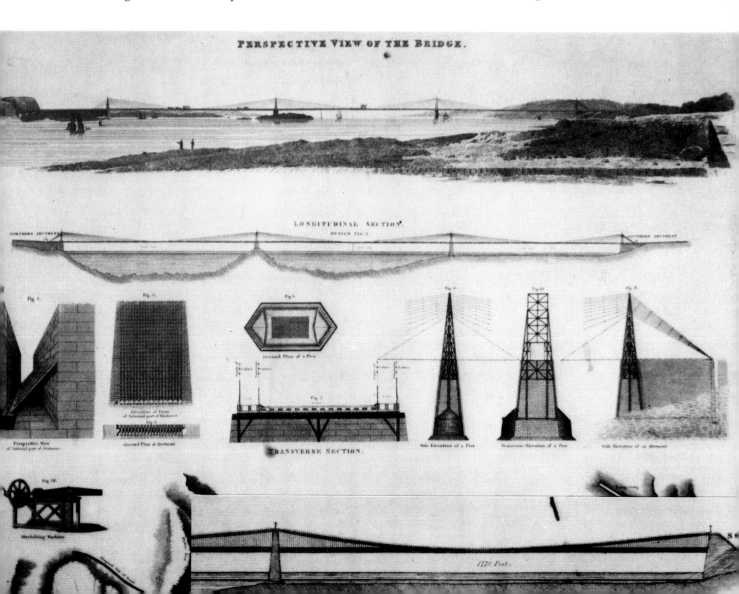

Fig. 1.17. Proposed
'chain' bridge at
Queensferry, Anderson
1818: plan at south side;
(inset) chain and cable
details

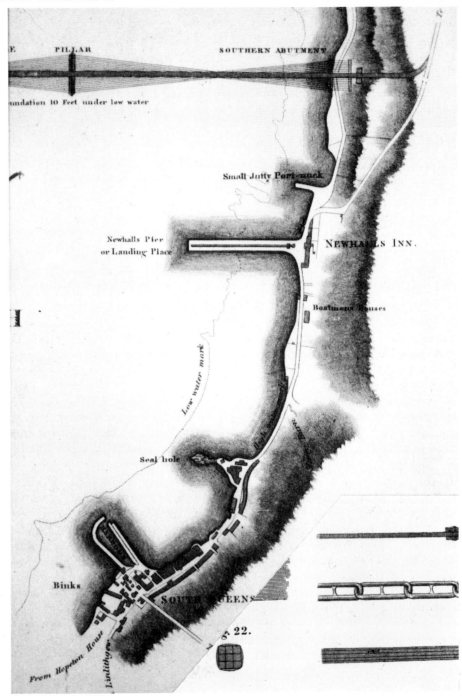

Road bridge schemes

Possible Roman campaign boat bridge

A bridge across the Forth at Queensferry was probably considered by the Romans, possibly *c.* 208 during the campaigns of Emperor Severus and his son Caracalla. One Romanist has recently suggested that a 1¼ mile long boat bridge, secured to long mooring ropes and divided near its middle by Inchgarvie, was constructed under the guidance of Caracalla about where the Forth Bridge now stands (Fig. 1.14).[35] In the absence of firm evidence the case for such a bridge is conjectural, but the Romans did have the technology, men, and access to materials to have built one. There are various precedents of boat bridges elsewhere; some are depicted on Trajan's column. Several tens of thousands of Roman soldiers are believed to have campaigned north of the Forth, and a bridge would have formed a useful link northward from the Severan base at Cramond 3 miles to the east. It is difficult to imagine a boat bridge surviving winter storms; it was possibly assembled seasonally or for particular operations. The provision, positioning and securing of some 500 boats would have been a major task. Would the Romans have given such a project priority over a ferrying operation?

Developments 1740–1817

A bridge may have been suggested as early as 1740[24] or 1758,[36] but no details have been found. As the materials then available for construction were essentially timber and stone, with limitations in use on bridge spans of about 100 ft and a maximum foundation depth of about 10–15 ft under shallow water, a bridge in deep water would have been impracticable. In 1772 Smeaton thought it would be worth spending up to £100 000 (perhaps equivalent to £50 million today) to bridge the Forth at Queensferry, but considered a bridge infeasible.[4] The considerably increased production of good quality wrought iron that followed implementation of Henry Cort's inventions in iron manufacture after 1783 gave engineers scope for constructing bridges with tension members. Before Cort's improvements, a tilt hammer working by water power produced 1 ton of bars of doubtful quality in 12 hours. His rolling mill, absorbing approximately the same power, produced 15 tons of uniformly high quality iron in the same time. At the final stage, the iron was passed through grooved rollers to produce uniform sections of various dimensions (Fig. 1.15)[37] The wrought iron link-bar suspension bridge was adopted in North America from 1800.[39] Telford designed an arch bridge for crossing Menai Strait with centering supported by inclined iron stays. By August 1817 Scotland probably led Europe in having four iron tension footbridges erected. Their spans ranged from 110 to 261 ft.[40] From 1814–17 Telford and Captain Samuel Brown (1774–1852) were taking the first steps in developing the long-span suspension bridge for carriage traffic based on experiments for the Runcorn Bridge project.[41] At the end of 1817 the first practical 'strength of materials' textbook having any bearing on the subject was published, dealing mainly with timber.[42]

Anderson's 'Chain Bridge' designs, (January 1818)

It was against this primitive technological background that an Edinburgh land surveyor, civil engineer and former pupil of Jardine, James Anderson (*c.* 1790–1861), proposed a wrought iron suspension bridge on either the rod-stay or catenarian bar-cable principle (Fig. 1.16).[43] He envisaged spans of 2000 ft, with estimated costs for alternative heights of 90 and 110 ft above the river of £144 000–205 000. The site was to have been within about 300 yards of the present rail bridge (Fig. 1.17). The headroom for shipping was to have been 90 or 110 ft, and the deck 33 ft wide with a 25 ft carriageway. In the rod-stay design the pairs of rods terminated at the outside of the deck at 100 ft (or 50 ft) intervals, and at the other end fanned out laterally across the tower top to counteract 'the effects of wind and any undulating or vibratory motion'. The stays were to have had cross-sectional areas proportional to the strain induced. The pair of stays from the tower tops to mid-span would have a declination of 100 ft in 1000 ft, just less than 6°.

For the catenarian cable or alternative design a curvature depth of one-thirtieth of the chord line (66 ft 4 inches) was proposed. Twelve 3 inch nominal diameter cables were envisaged, each consisting of nine ⅝ inch square bars and four facing segments, the whole bound round with wire (Fig. 1.17). For this proposal the iron stays of the first design were retained to inhibit deck undulation. In both designs masonry piers were proposed with

Fig. 1.18. Iron strength testing arrangement by Anderson (after Telford) (Ref. 42)

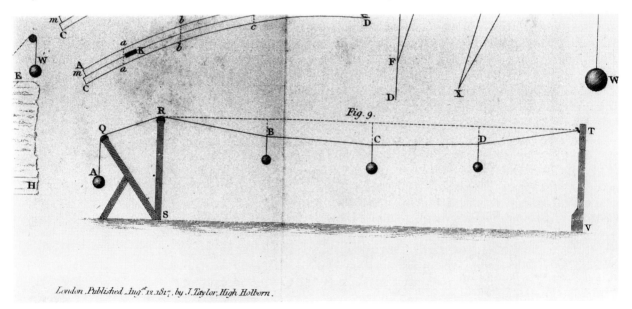

London Published Aug.ᵗ 12.1817. by J.Taylor, High Holborn.

Fig. 1.19. Trinity Pier, Newhaven: seaward abutment 1821 (Ref. 48)

Fig. 1.20. Dee Bridge, Chester 1847: combined cast and wrought iron girder bridge with 100 ft spans (Ref. 52)

cast iron tower frames above the roadway. The timber deck was to have rested on 20 (or for the stay design 40) principal bar members or 'basis chains' 1 × 1½ inches deep extending nearly 600 ft between abutments and tensioned to a sag of 20 ft in 2000 ft. The abutments and towers were to have been constructed first, over which was to have been stretched a temporary catenarian footway along which the stays to meet at mid-span would have been conducted. The middle bearer with two 'basis chains' was then to have been hoisted up from boats and the stay ends connected.

The cables and bars were to have been stretched into position using a machine capable of exerting 65 tons from 1 cwt applied to the handle, and to terminate at a cast iron anchor beam on each side of the bridge. These anchors were to have been positioned 150 ft behind each abutment face and 100 ft below the roadway, stability being provided by a superincumbent mass of masonry of these dimensions 40 ft wide and weighing nearly 23 000 tons. Anderson based his proposed ironwork on simple experimental results (Fig. 1.18), both his own and Telford's, and assumed a design proportionality factor of 15–20 tons/in^2, or half of what he presumed to be its breaking strain. He proposed using local stone and 'excellent quality' lime from the Elgin Lime Works. Anderson particularly emphasised the need for further experiments on a larger scale before deciding a preference for either design, and 'reserved the right to modify and improve them.[43] He sent copies of his designs to Telford,[44] who almost certainly regarded them as over-ambitious.

Assessment

At the time of publication of his designs Anderson was probably about 26 years of age, with more experience of land surveying than civil engineering. His designs as illustrated were undoubtedly over-ambitious for the technology of his time, and later evoked Westhofen's understandable and well-known comment that the proposed structure was 'so light indeed that on a dull day it would hardly have been visible and after a heavy gale probably no longer to be seen on a clear day either'.[45] Basically, the cross-sectional areas of the iron cables and bars were much too small for the elevations adopted, which, with tower heights of only 67 and 100 ft above the roadway, were too flat. Unacceptably high levels of stress would have been induced in the ironwork. Anderson seems to have been unaware that as wrought iron was stretched, it deformed permanently beyond a stress of between 9.5 and 11.5 tons/in^2;[46] the stress in the cables of his catenarian design would have exceeded these figures under their self-weight alone. His design stress was three to four times greater than the 5 tons/in^2 value for wrought iron which gained general acceptance later. The provision against deck oscillation was also inadequate, but at least some allowance had been made. Even at that time Telford regarded 1000 ft as a maximum span for suspension bridges, modifying this to 800 ft after experiencing deck oscillation at Menai Bridge in 1825 and to 600 ft for the high crossing of Clifton Gorge. It was not until 1931, with the completion of George Washington Bridge, that a 2000 ft span was actually attained and surpassed.

The nearest Anderson seems to have come to suspension bridge construction was the successful renewal in 1830 of the timber seaward abutment of Trinity Chain Pier, erected by Captain Samuel Brown for steamboat use in 1821 (Fig. 1.19).[47,48] This was a difficult and hazardous operation, entailing the replacement of many sea-worm ravaged piles while preserving the tension supporting the structure.

It is doubtful whether Anderson would have promoted his designs at all if he had not been encouraged by Telford's Runcorn Bridge project with its 1000 ft central span.[49,50] Unfortunately for him, Telford's development of the long-span suspension bridge had not yet matured and been translated into

Fig. 1.21 (facing page, top left) Britannia Bridge, Menai Strait: tube construction 1848; note the two extra compression webs at the top to equalize with the tensile strength in the bottom

Fig. 1.22 (facing page, top right) Sir Thomas Bouch (Ref. 62)

Fig. 1.23. (facing page, bottom) Forth Floating Railway, Bouch 1850: Granton slipway

the elegant and long-lasting Menai Bridge, a process which took a further 5 years to evolve at the frontiers of technology. In consequence, Anderson adopted and even compounded undesirable features from the 1814 Runcorn bridge design which Telford later abandoned, e.g. the cable form which was then premature, catenarian cables of too flat a curvature under as well as over the roadway, and a design stress that was too high.[51]

Finally, Anderson deserves some credit for correctly foreseeing rock-founded cable-stayed or suspension bridges as the means of achieving the greatest spans. The proposal helped to establish his reputation and he went on to develop a notable harbour engineering practice in Edinburgh, and in 1836 was elected FRSE.

Railway bridges

From 1830–50 most iron bridges on railways were of the cast iron arch or beam types or combinations of cast and wrought iron, the latter contributing additional tensile support, with spans rarely exceeding 100 ft (Fig. 1.20)[52] A number of failures involving cast iron beams had occurred; from the mid-century wrought iron generally replaced cast iron for use in beams, but not in arches until towards the end of the century. The wrought iron plate girder, precursor of the steel 'I' beam, developed *c.* 1846. A railway suspension bridge erected at Stockton in 1830 was under-designed and proved hopelessly inadequate, two wagons causing a deflection of 18 inches; after being propped for a time it was replaced by a cast iron bridge in 1842.[41] This experience discouraged engineers from adopting suspension bridges for railways. The Menai Tubular Bridge with its 460 ft spans and correctly strength-proportioned sections, constructed from 1846–50 under the super-intendence of Stephenson and Fairbairn with assistance from Hodgkinson, represented a major step forward in the evolution of the wrought iron girder bridge (Fig. 1.21).[53] Crossing the Forth and Tay was a bigger challenge, and a less satisfactory, although enterprising, interim solution was adopted by Sir Thomas Bouch (1822–80) (Fig. 1.22). By 1850 he had designed and success-fully installed the world's first floating railway between Granton and Burntisland.

The Granton–Burntisland 'Floating Railway' (1850)

The ferry vessel was a specially designed end-loading paddle-steamer called Leviathan, built by Robert Napier & Co. The 389 ton vessel had a speed of 5 knots and commenced operation in February 1850. It could carry up to 34 goods wagons; the average time for a single trip, including loading and unloading an average of 21 wagons, was 56 minutes.[54] The wagon transference arrangement on each shore consisted of a slipway travelling platform with horizontal top, at the end of which were four movable wrought iron girders to be lowered on to the end of the ferry boat when the platform was in position. The platform was moved up and down the slipway by means

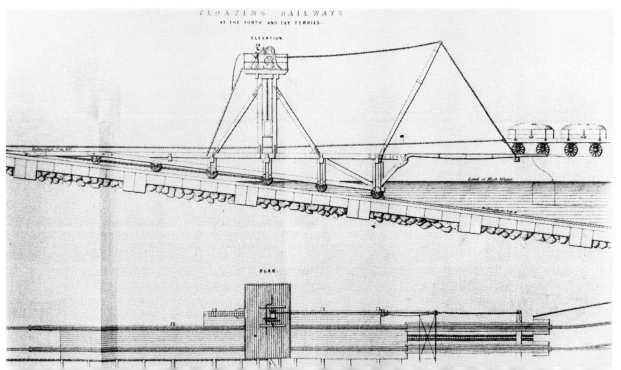

FLOATING RAILWAYS
AT THE FORTH AND TAY FERRIES.

ELEVATION

Level of High Water

PLAN

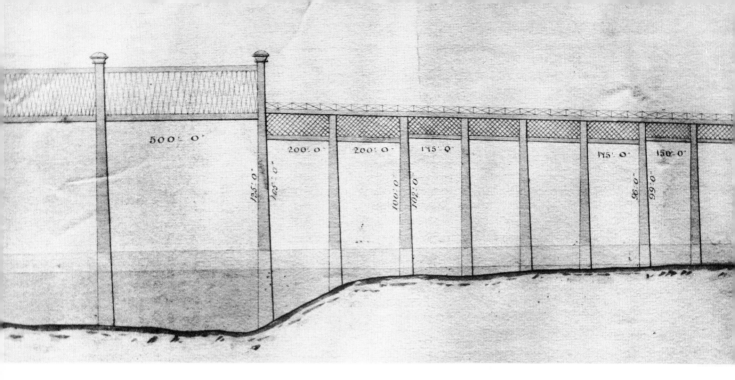

500' 0"

125' 0"

165' 0"

200' 0" 200' 0" 145' 0"

100' 0"

102' 0"

145' 0" 150' 0"

96' 0"

99' 0"

Fig. 1.24. Proposed Forth Bridge, Charlestown: Bouch 1865 (Ref. 61)

of a 30 hp stationary steam engine that was also used to land the trains. The movable girders were operated manually from two powerful crab-winches above the platform (Fig. 1.23).[55] In the early 1860s Bouch proposed a similar system at Queensferry to accommodate passenger trains, but allowed his preference for a bridge to override this concept which he considered comparatively inefficient. The Granton to Burntisland railway ferry continued to operate until the Forth Bridge was opened in 1890.

Bouch credited Thomas Grainger (1794–1852), his predecessor as Engineer to the Edinburgh, Perth and Dundee Railway, with the original idea of floating trains across the Forth. Grainger proposed to use hydraulic cranes to transfer trains between shore and the ferry vessel—Bouch thought that this operation would be too slow. Another engineer, J. F. Bateman (1810–89) claimed that he had originated the floating train concept with a proposal for Queensferry in 1845 when he was Engineer to the Edinburgh and Perth Railway. He had proposed installing stationary steam engines at the top of 1 in 12 ramps on each shore, trains being hauled over tailpieces between the vessel and ramp.[55]

The proposed Forth bridge at Charlestown (1862–66)
Bouch, now Engineer of the North British and Edinburgh and Glasgow Railways, first considered the Queensferry site for a bridge across the Forth. He ruled out a suspension bridge there as being inappropriate for railway traffic, and rejected a girder bridge on account of the impracticability of

founding piers in up to 240 ft of water and because of the impediment to navigation.[56] The predisposition against using suspension bridges for railway traffic was not accepted by all engineers. In 1864 a 'Mr Thorntan of Edinburgh', probably Robert Thornton, prepared plans for a suspension bridge with three 2000 ft spans at or near the site of the present railway bridge.[57] In 1862, a Charles Dowling published a proposal for a bridge with two continuous wrought iron tubes 5810 ft long in seven 800 ft spans at about the same site. Although he considered the tubes to be just selfsupporting at this span, he proposed adding suspension chains or cables, including some diagonals, to inhibit lateral movement.[58] Neither of these proposals was adopted.

In 1862 the Westminster consultant engineers G. R. Stephenson (1819–1905) and J. F. Tone[59] produced an outline report for consideration by the North British Railway directors on the means by which it might be possible to 'pass' the River Forth. Stephenson had already had the experience of constructing a major iron bridge over the Nile, and had assisted his eminent cousin Robert Stephenson with the multispan box girder bridge over the St Lawrence at Montreal. Stephenson and Tone strongly advised against the railway ferry concept, which they considered inefficient. They also advised against the construction of a bridge across the Forth at Queensferry, considering a suspension bridge with minimum spans of 1300 ft to be impracticable for railway traffic, and cited the speed limit of 3 mph on the American engineer J. A. Roebling's 800 ft span Niagara Bridge (1855–97) (Fig. 2.2, p. 38). Stephenson and Tone recommended construction of an iron girder bridge across the Forth between Blackness Castle and Charlestown at an estimated cost of £500 000 and completion time of 3 years.[59]

Bouch seems to have accepted or reached the same conclusions as Stephenson and Tone, and in 1863–64 was working on designs for a single-track girder bridge across the Forth near Charlestown. One design in 1864 was for a 3979 yard viaduct rising to 100 ft in height for two 290 ft navigation spans. From the south the spans were (in ft) 19 × 40, 42 × 40, 24 × 207, 2 × 290, 4 × 207, 44 × 40 and 4 × 40.[60] Another design had spans ranging from 100 ft to two of 600 ft over the navigation channel.[56] The proposed main spans were larger than those of Britannia Bridge, and of Brunel's Saltash Bridge (1859) with its 455 ft spans. The company prevailed on Bouch to reduce the large spans, and the design for the 'Bridge of Forth' in the 1865 Bill was a 3887 yard viaduct with 62 wrought iron close-lattice girder spans, rising to 125 ft clearance for four 500 ft navigation spans. From the south end the spans were (in ft): 14 × 100, 6 × 150, 6 × 175, 15 × 200, 4 × 500, 2 × 200, 4 × 173, 4 × 150 and 7 × 100 (Fig. 1.24).[61] The 500 ft span girders, each 64 ft deep and weighing 1170 tons, were to have been fabricated on land, floated to site on pontoons and elevated into position by means of hydraulic jacks. The bridge was estimated to cost £476 000, excluding the railway and contin-

Fig. 1.25. Proposed Forth Bridge, Charlestown: Bouch 1865, cross-section drawn on 1881 newspaper cutting showing old and present Tay Bridges (Ref. 68)

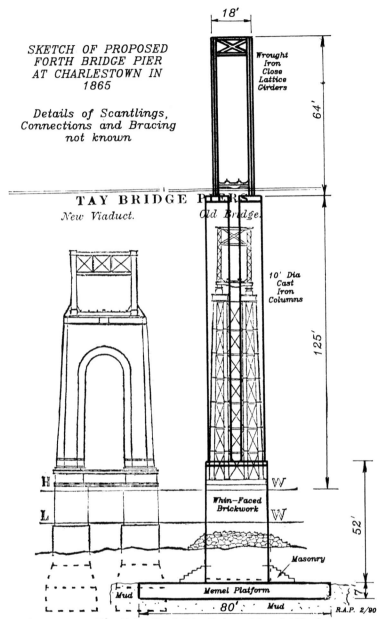

SKETCH OF PROPOSED
FORTH BRIDGE PIER
AT CHARLESTOWN IN
1865

*Details of Scantlings,
Connections and Bracing
not known*

18'

Wrought
Iron
Close
Lattice
Girders

64'

TAY BRIDGE PIERS

New Viaduct.   *Old Bridge.*

10' Dia
Cast
Iron
Columns

125'

H   W

L   W

Whin—Faced
Brickwork

52'

Masonry

Mud   Memel Platform   Mud   7

80'   R.A.P. 2/90

We are indebted to Messrs Barlow, Son, & Baker, Engineers of the undertaking, for the sketch reproduced above of the Cross Section of the new Viaduct, showing the relative positions of the new work and the old Bridge. The massive character of the new structure as compared with the old is obvious at a glance, especially (1) the greater lateral stability from the substitution of twin piers for the single pier below, and the increased width for the double line of rails above ; and (2) the greater vertical stability from the diminished height of the superstructure and the arched formation at the upper junction of the piers.

gencies. If it had been built it would have been the longest and largest railway bridge in the world.

The promoters were concerned about the difficulty of achieving adequate foundations for the great girder piers in soft ground. Of the many borings made on Bouch's behalf by Jesse Wylie (whose subsequent borings for the Tay Bridge indicated a non-existent rock shelf almost right across river, and involved Bouch in fundamental design changes and considerable delay),[62] many easily penetrated through soft silt for more than 120 ft. One bore even went to 231 ft without reaching the bottom.[23] Several hundred borings showed not a single bit of stone.[56] In 1864 Bouch conducted experiments on site to determine the bearing capacity of the ground in the river bed using two 6 ft diameter cylinders 48 ft high, one with an open end and the other with a closed end. After loading with 60 tons of pig iron one cylinder became top heavy and toppled over. On 7 November 1864 another cylinder was successfully loaded with 80 tons, and was expected to take 120 tons or 'if possible 5 tons/ft^2' later that day.[64] This outcome encouraged Bouch to proceed.

In 1865 the project was examined at length by parliamentary referees before the Act came into force. Bouch explained in evidence that he proposed to determine whether satisfactory foundations could be obtained for the piers of the large girders by building and load testing an experimental pier in situ. He proposed reducing the pressure on the mud to less than 0·75 ton/ft^2 by use of a platform of green beech 114 ft × 80 ft × 9 ft thick, which being slightly denser than seawater would sink without load. This was to be towed to site supported by floats and sunk into position. On top of the platform the masonry and brickwork were to be built up within a wrought iron cylinder to 12 ft above high-water level as the platform sank into position in the mud in 40 ft of water. Twelve 8 ft diameter tubes on the platform around the edge of the masonry and also the interior cavity of the piers were to be loaded with 10 000 tons of pig iron, equivalent to 2½ times the weight of the structure plus a standing train. The piers above the brickwork were to consist of a pair of 10 ft diameter cast iron columns 1 inch thick (Fig. 1.25).[56,63] Bouch envisaged the girder spans as continuous but had not so designed them, considering this an additional safety factor.

On 14 June 1866, Bouch's trial platform was launched from Burntisland and towed into position off Charlestown. It was smaller than previously conceived, now being 80 ft × 60 ft × 7 ft thick and constructed of memel (pine).[63] Six weeks later, when preparations for submersion of the platform were rapidly approaching completion, the company suddenly abandoned the project, apparently for financial reasons. It is understood that it expected to lose northern 'through traffic' revenue following an amalgamation between their Caledonian Railway rival and the Scottish North Eastern Railway, on 10 August 1866.[66,67] The workmen were paid off and the raft was towed back to

Fig. 1.26. Runcorn Bridge today: constructed 1863–68

Burntisland, the experiment having cost the North British Railway Company £34 390.[67]

Assessment of the Charlestown Bridge proposal of 1865–6

With hindsight, the abandonment of the bridge was almost certainly cheap at the price, as its design did not allow a sufficient margin of safety for resisting strong winds. Also, its questionable structural continuity vertically from edge of foundation base to lattice girder and its raft foundations resting on 'mud'[60] would both have been unacceptable in modern design terms. Although the proposal survived close parliamentary scrutiny, the wind problem was not properly appreciated at the time. Bouch envisaged a wind load of 180 tons on a 500 ft span, weighing 1170 tons, based on a pressure of 30 lbs/ft². The composition of the lattice girder elevation is not known, but it is reasonable to assume that it consisted of 58% holes and 42% iron on the basis that the wind pressure was applied to the net area of iron. The girder design was probably influenced by Runcorn Bridge (1863) (Fig. 1.26).[63] Bouch would probably also have adopted a factor of safety against overturning.

If the rules drawn up by the Board of Trade Committee immediately after the Tay Bridge disaster[69] had applied to this proposal, i.e. 56 lbs/ft^2 on the windward and 28 lbs/ft^2 on the leeward side of the girder, the design wind load would have been 1200 tons, based on the gross area of the girder discounting the holes. In addition, the committee specified a factor of safety of 2 against overturning where gravity provided the restoring force, and a factor of safety of 4 was to be applied to holding down connections resisting overturning. Modern practice would give a design wind load of 580 tonnes, more than three times the figure that Bouch estimated, and a minimum factor of safety to be applied to this against overturning of 1·4. A comparison of these figures indicates the considerable over-reaction by the Committee to the wind question subsequent to the Tay Bridge disaster. Both figures, however, are greatly in excess of the 180 tons assumed by Bouch. The design is also questionable from the standpoint of post-construction settlement, even if the experimental foundation had been successful initially.

Fig. 1.27. Forth Suspension Bridge proposal: Bouch 1873

Bouch's design, if implemented, would not necessarily have engendered a great Forth Bridge failure of 1869, similar to the fate of the Tay Bridge a decade later—the former's piers were more robust, and the design might have been substantially modified before construction. Without details of the scantlings, connection arrangements and bracings it is not possible to comment with certainty as to how the different elements of the design would have fared under various loadings. However, when compared with the present Tay Bridge of similar length completed in 1889, with its iron caissons sunk at least 20 ft into the sandy silt, widely straddled piers, and compliance with the post-disaster wind pressure code, there is no doubt which design is preferable.

The Forth railway suspension bridge project (1871–80)
The pressure in favour of bridging the Forth and Tay did not subside for long. Under new management, the North British Railway Company took over the ferry at Queensferry in 1867. In 1868 the railway from Ratho Junction to Queensferry was completed, thus establishing a rail–ferry link with Fife. This link was further developed in 1877–78 with the construction at Queensferry of a 900 ft timber jetty and a 1300 ft whinstone breakwater.

In 1871, Bouch prepared several designs[45] and proposed a double span steel suspension bridge with heavily stiffened deck and 1600 ft spans more or less on the line of the present bridge (Fig. 1.27). Having been carefully examined and favourably reported on by the eminent engineers W. H. Barlow (1812–1902) and W. Pole (1814–1900),[70] the bridge was granted its authorising Act in August 1873. Work was slow to start, and it was not until 30 September 1878 that the foundation stone of a brick pier was laid at Inchgarvie. Towards the end of 1879 William Arrol (1839–1913) was hard at work on preparations for the steelwork when the Tay Bridge fell. Confidence in Bouch evaporated, and within about a year his design had been abandoned. A still surviving, rather sad epitaph is the score or so courses of Inchgarvie pier's brickwork, now supporting a small iron lighthouse (Fig. 2.4, p. 40).

Bouch may have been influenced to change his mind and adopt a suspension bridge by the success of Roebling's Cincinnati–Covington road suspension bridge. This bridge of 1075 ft span was completed in 1866 and is still in use.[71] It is intriguing to reflect that if the piers of the Tay Bridge had not failed, the Forth might be spanned by a twin suspension bridge instead of our present masterpiece. For a modern assessment of the practicability of Bouch's design, see Chapter 2.

Acknowledgements

The Author acknowledges with gratitude much appreciated assistance received from members of staff of the ICE Library, the National Library of Scotland, the Royal Society and the Scottish Record Office; the Earl of Elgin and Kincardine; Hopetoun House Preservation Trust; Mr P. Cadell; Mr D.

Cameron; Mr C. Johnston; Mr W. T. Johnston; Mr A. Loughlin; Dr G. Maxwell; Mrs S. Purves; Mr J. S. Shipway; Professor A. W. Skempton; Mr C. J. Smith; Mrs M. Young; and Elton Engineering Books.

References

1. *Extracts from the Records of the Convention of the Royal Burghs of Scotland 1759–79*. Pillans and Wilson, Edinburgh, 1918.
2. *Minutes of the Commissioners of Forfeited Estates 1745*. 1768–82, Scottish Record Office manuscript E721/11.
3. Skempton A. W. *John Smeaton FRS*. Thomas Telford, London, 1981.
4. Smeaton J. Report on Queensferry Shipping Places, 15 August 1772, in *Reports of the late John Smeaton*. London, 1837, 2nd edn.
5. Smeaton J. *Reports of the late John Smeaton*. 1837, Vol. 2, 123.
6. Mason J. *The story of the water passage at Queensferry*. W. Denny and Bros, Dumbarton, 1962.
7. Graham A. Archaeological notes on some harbours in eastern Scotland. *Proc. Soc. Antiq. Scot.*, 1968–69, 101.
8. 49. Geo. III. c. 83.
9. Boucher C. G. T. *John Rennie 1761–1821*. Manchester, 1963.
10. *Statement respecting the Queen's-Ferry Passage and the Great North Road*, London, 1811.
11. 54. Geo. III. c. 138.
12. *Edinburgh Advertiser*, 13 April 1816.
13. Letter from John Paterson to John Rennie, 29 October 1817. National Library of Scotland, manuscript 19795.
14. Brodie I. *Queensferry Passage*. West Lothian History and Amenity Society, 1976.
15. Stevenson R. Origin of steam-boats and description of Stevenson's Dalswinton steam-boat. *Annals of Philosophy*, April 1819, XIII.
16. Telford T. *Report on the Queensferry Passage*, in *Report of the Committee appointed by the Managing Trustees of the Queensferry Passage on the fifth April 1828*. Edinburgh (?).
17. Telford T. *Report respecting the Lower Ferry between the Counties of Midlothian and Fife*. Edinburgh, 1828.
18. Tredgold T. *A practical essay on the strength of cast iron*. London, 1822.
19. Taylor J. *The Pennyles pilgrimage*. London, 1618, reprinted in *The Old Book Collector's Miscellany*, ed. Ch. Hindley, London, 1872.
20. Shaw J. *Water power in Scotland 1550–1870*. John Donald, Edinburgh, 1984.
21. Agricola G. *De Re Metallica*. Basileae, 1556.
22. Communicated to the author by The Earl of Elgin and Kincardine.
23. Cadell H. M. *The Story of the Forth*. Maclehose, Glasgow, 1913, 81–103.
24 *History of the Forth Bridge*. Banks & Co., Edinburgh, 1911.

25. Grieve J. *et al. Reports of surveys made for ascertaining the practicability of making a land tunnel under the River Forth*. Edinburgh, 1806.
26. *Scots Magazine* August, 1806.
27. Miller J. and Vazie W. *Observations on the advantages and practicability of making tunnels under navigable rivers, particularly applicable to the proposed tunnel under the Forth*. Edinburgh, 1807.
28. The Kinneil Valleyfield link up. *Colliery Engineering*, December 1964.
29. Francis E. H. and Armstrong, M. *The geology of the Stirling district*, HMSO, London, 1970, 263.
30. James J. G. Ralph Dodd, the very ingenious schemer. *Trans. Newcomen Soc.*, 1976, **47.**
31. Dodd R. *Reports . . . of the proposed dry tunnel . . . from Gravesend in Kent to Tilbury in Essex*. London, 1798.
32. Law H. A Memoir of the Thames Tunnel 1824. *Quarterly Papers on Engineering*, ed. J. Weale, London, 1844–49.
33. Beamish R. *Memoir of the life of Sir Marc Isambard Brunel*. London, 1862.
34. Clements P. *Marc Isambard Brunel*. London, 1970.
35. Reed N. The Scottish campaigns of Septimius Severus. *Proc. Soc. Antiq. Scot*, 1975–76, **107**, 96–102.
36. Weir M. *Ferries in Scotland*. John Donald, Edinburgh, 1988.
37. Pannell J. P. M. *An illustrated history of Civil Engineering*. London, 1964.
38. *The National Cyclopaedia*. Undated, 1847–59?
39. Paxton R. A. Menai Bridge (1818–26) and its influence on suspension bridge development. *Trans. Newcomen Soc.*, 1977–78, 49.
40. Stevenson R. Description of bridges of suspension. *Edin. Phil. J.*, Apr.–Oct. 1821, **V**.
41. Paxton R. A. The influence of Thomas Telford . . . on the use of improved constructional materials in Civil Engineering practice. Heriot–Watt University, Edinburgh, MSc thesis, 1975.
42. Barlow P. *An essay on the strength and stress of timber*. Also an appendix on *The strength of iron*, London, 1817.
43. Anderson J. *Plan and sections of a bridge of chains proposed to be thrown over the Firth of Forth at Queensferry*. Edinburgh, 1818.
44. Institution of Civil Engineers' copy.
45. Westhofen W. *The Forth Bridge*. London, 1890. *Engineering*, 28 Feb. 1890.
46. Kirkaldy W. G. Illustrations of David Kirkaldy's system of mechanical testing. London, 1891.
47. *Report from the Select Committee . . . Harbours of Leith and Newhaven with the Minutes of Evidence*. House of Commons, 6 July 1835.
48. Brown Captain S. Description of the Trinity Pier. *Edin. Phil. J.*, 1822, **VI**.
49. Telford T. *Report of Select Committee . . . proposed bridge at Runcorn*. 13 March 1817, Warrington.
50. Telford T. *Report of Select Committee . . . proposed bridge at Runcorn*. Supplementary report, 22 July 1817.

51. Paxton R. A. Menai Bridge 1818–26. *Thomas Telford: Engineer*. Thomas Telford, London, 1980.
52. *Illustrated London News*, 12 June 1847.
53. Clark E. *The Britannia and Conway tubular bridges*. London, 1850.
54. Scott W. *The railways of Fife*. Melven Press, Perth, 1980.
55. Hall W. On the floating railways across the Forth and Tay Ferries in connection with the Edinburgh, Perth and Dundee Railway. *Min. Proc. ICE*, 1861–2, **XX**.
56. Referees on private bills . . . North British and Edinburgh and Glasgow (Bridge of Forth) Railway Bill 8 May 1865. *Minutes of evidence*. House of Commons, SRO BR/PYB/(S)/1/36.
57. *Engineer*, 29 April 1864, **17**, 258.
58. Dowling C. H. Iron work: practical Formulae . . . with the description of a suggested Railway Bridge across the Queensferry. Forms Div. II of *Formulae, Rules, and Examples for Candidates for the Military, Naval, and Civil Service Examinations*. London, Weale, 1826.
59. Stephenson G. R. and Tone J. F. *Report on Firth of Forth Bridge*, London, 1862.
60. *Forth Bridge railway plan shewing bores on site of proposed viaduct*. 1864, Elgin Estates Archives.
61. *Cartoon Forth and Tay Bridges*. 1865, Elgin Estates Archives.
62. Prebble J. *The high girders*. London, 1956.
63. *Scotsman*, 14 June 1866.
64. Thomas J. Scotland, the Lowlands and Borders. *A Regional History of the Railways of Great Britain*, Vol. 6, Newton Abbot, 1971.
65. *Scotsman*, 6 August 1866.
66. Bradshaw's railway manual, London, 1874.
67. Douglas H. *Crossing the Forth*. Robert Hale, London, 1964.
68. *Dundee Advertiser*, 18 October 1881.
69. Barlow C. *The New Tay Bridge*. London, 1889.
70. Barlow W. H. and Pole W. *Report on the Forth Bridge, designed by Thomas Bouch*. Edinburgh, 1880.
71. Roebling J. A. *Annual Report of the . . . Covington & Cincinnati Bridge Company*. Trenton, 1867. Bridge illustrated on cover of ASCE calendar 1990.

Additional sources

Skempton A. W. *British Civil Engineering 1640–1840: a bibliography*. Mansell, London, 1987.
Marshall J. *A biographical dictionary of Railway Engineers*. David and Charles, Newton Abbot, 1978.
Dictionary of National Biography, Oxford University Press.

CHAPTER 2

Design of the bridge

J. S. Shipway, *R. H. Cuthbertson and Partners, Consulting Engineers*

The nature of design

In civil and structural engineering the term 'design' is often used without strict observance of its true meaning. Sometimes we use it when we mean calculation or analysis of a structure, but in reality a structure is analysed and calculated only after the design has been chosen, however tentatively. The design of a structure is its form, its shape, its basic concept. When this is decided, calculations are made to establish whether it can be constructed, and to estimate the cost. This is only the start of the design process. The analysis and calculation check may mean many revisions, or the scrapping of the initial idea altogether and a new start. The path of engineering design is often, therefore, a slow, irregular and halting journey: sometimes, however, the right solution emerges at the start and little adjustment is required, depending on how inspired the designer happens to be.[1]

The ability to foresee difficulties and advantages in the realization or construction of the design is essential to the process. This requires experience as well as insight and understanding. There is a close connection between the idea and the means of achieving it—the engineer must have a knowledge of how things are constructed and made.[2]

Civil engineering has advanced throughout the years in the employment of new materials and new technology as they have been developed, and in the understanding of the behaviour of structures through analysis and calculation. In general, a design should make the most of available technology, but it will also be limited and influenced by available technology, including the materials available. The design must engender the confidence of the user—this was a major difficulty after the collapse of the Tay Bridge in 1879. Obviously, a design should represent value for money, although in the past many a white elephant has eluded capture or escaped unnoticed until it was too late. All these factors must be carefully assessed and weighed; they generate and influence the form of the design.

Bridge design

Two aspects of design, then, are the conception of the idea and its realisation

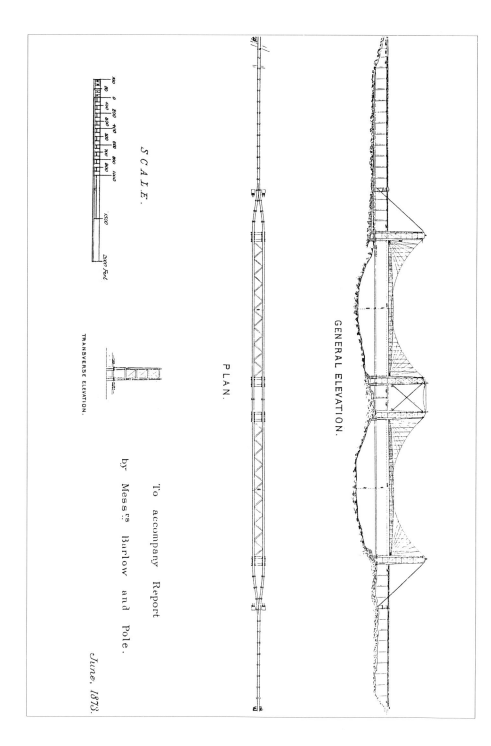

Fig. 2.1. Proposed Forth Bridge by Thomas Bouch, 1873

Fig. 2.2. Suspension bridge carrying rail traffic: Roebling, 1855

Fig. 2.3. (facing page) Alternative designs for the Forth Bridge by Thomas Bouch: (bottom) forces in chains and diagonals

in material form. In bridge design, further aspects are function, safety and economy; and above all, the means of construction. The fulfilment of every requirement can entail many conflicting demands.

Function

A bridge is built for a purpose and must fulfil its function—in the case in question, the carrying of a double line of railway across the Forth. It is subject to heavy loads, the influence of weather, a corrosive marine atmosphere, metal fatigue, temperature changes and perhaps accident. Durability and serviceability over many years are expected—this has come to mean 120 years in the case of a railway bridge.

Safety

There are two aspects of safety in bridge design. First, when completed and ready for use the bridge must be safe, and must fulfil its function with a sufficient margin of safety to engender confidence and trust. Second, the structure has to be safe during its construction. Many bridges have collapsed or fallen while being built, and we do not need to be reminded that mishaps

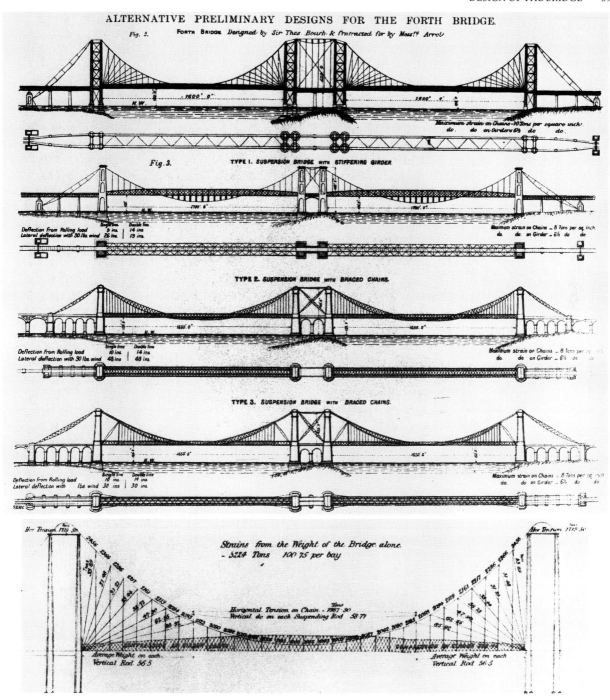

ALTERNATIVE PRELIMINARY DESIGNS FOR THE FORTH BRIDGE.

continue to the present day.

During the design of the Forth Bridge the memory of the Tay Bridge disaster loomed large in the public mind, and safety was of paramount importance. A design not only had to be safe; it had to *look* safe. Hence the heavily plated pier legs of the present Tay railway bridge—they had to look substantial as well as being so.

Construction

The choice of method has a big influence on time and cost, and the exigencies of site construction dominate many decisions in the design of a bridge. In a bridge site such as the Forth there is maximum exposure to wind and weather, it is over open water, which is extremely deep in places, and suitable places for foundations are few and far between. Further, safety must prevail at all stages of construction. These problems are inescapable; the design must overcome them all.

Economy

The search to achieve the desired design for the minimum expenditure of human effort (of which money is the best measure) is never-ending. The pursuit of economy requires early consideration of the means of construction, and this applies from the base of the foundations to the final coat of paint. Economy is often obtained by simplicity of construction.

To sum up, in the preparation of a bridge design much talent and experience is required. Its execution will engage large numbers of men, much construction plant, and large sums of money. Very heavy responsibilities are

Fig. 2.4. Remains of Bouch bridge abandoned in 1881

involved; the bigger the bridge, the greater the responsibility. The spans necessary to cross the Forth were almost four times as large as any railway bridge previously constructed in the UK, which as yet had no cantilever bridges—also, steel was an unknown material for bridge applications. The design and erection of these colossal spans was a mind-boggling and daunting task.

The Tay Bridge disaster and its aftermath

At this point it is necessary to touch briefly on the reasons for the fall of the first Tay Bridge and its influence on the design of the Forth Bridge. The original Tay Bridge was built in the 1870s and designed by Thomas Bouch, who was knighted for his work. He was a railway engineer of eminence, and had designed many structures for the North British and other railway companies in Scotland and the north of England. He had very considerable experience of bridges, and was at the peak of his fame when he designed the original Tay Bridge.

This bridge was to carry a single line of railway on brick piers throughout its two-mile length. However, owing to an inadequate site investigation, the rock on which the piers were to be founded was found not to exist for more than about one-sixth of the width of the crossing. This meant founding the remainder of the piers on sand—Bouch had to redesign them in cast iron columns and framing to lighten the load. The cast iron column work and the bracing were very poorly constructed; also, the bracing was designed to be of very light sections. In the gale of 28 December 1879 the bridge collapsed while a train was crossing the central navigation spans.

At the subsequent enquiry Bouch was found not to have made sufficient allowance for wind effects, in fact it is doubtful whether he made any at all. He had also failed to supervise the Contractor's castings of the columns sufficiently stringently, and the many defects in the castings had weakened the structure. The result was that the Board of Trade introduced new legislation stating that all bridges had to be designed for a lateral wind pressure of 56 lbs/ft^2. This severe figure was complied with fully in the design of the Forth Railway Bridge, which accounts partly for the shape of the structure and bracing.

The first Tay Bridge stood for only 18 months, but in the meantime Sir Thomas Bouch had been appointed to design the Forth Bridge, and construction had already begun. Following the collapse of the Tay Bridge, he was relieved of his appointment. Part of the first pier of his structure, however, still stands.

Early proposals—Bouch's bridge of 1873

A design for a bridge to span the Forth was prepared by Sir Thomas Bouch in the early 1870s (Fig. 2.1), and the first foundation pier was begun in 1878. Bouch was not the first engineer to prepare a design for this purpose, but his was the first design to reach the stage of construction, and was the first proposal for a railway bridge at Queensferry; previous proposals had been made for sites above and below Queensferry.

Bridging the Forth at Queensferry meant thinking big. In 1818, an Edinburgh civil engineer, James Anderson, startled the public with proposals for his suspension bridge with spans of 2000 ft, and the engineers for the present bridge gave Bouch the credit for the 'bold proposition to cross the Forth in two spans of 1600 ft'. Bouch's design must have been taking shape in his mind for many years before construction started, for its feasibility was the subject of a private independent report by two eminent engineers, W. H. Barlow and William Pole, as early as 1873.[3]

Suspension bridges are much more flexible than any other form of bridge. The cable or chain is the main support member—its curve distorts easily under uneven loading and causes disturbing oscillations and sag unless steps are taken to prevent it. This can be resisted by introducing stiffening, either of the chains themselves or by a deep braced girder forming the deck. These methods apply the loads to the chains in a more uniform manner, and reduce the deflection and distortion of the shape of the chain.

Bouch thought in terms of a stiffened suspension bridge to carry rail traffic. Many suspension bridges had been built to carry the road traffic of those days, which consisted mainly of horses and carts and carriages. This loading was very much lighter and more evenly distributed than the weight of a railway engine and a loaded train: in the 19th century only one stiffened suspension bridge to carry rail traffic was built—that over Niagara in the USA by Roebling in 1855 (Fig. 2.2). The span of the bridge was 821 ft, and it lasted for 42 years. In 1845 Stephenson planned to carry rail traffic over the Menai Straits by utilizing one side of the carriageway of Telford's suspension bridge. This idea proved impractical, and instead he developed the concept of the Menai tubular bridge, which was to incorporate suspension chains to assist the tubes in carrying the loads from rail traffic. However, it was found on further investigation that the massive tubes were sufficient to carry the rail loading by themselves, and the chains were never constructed, although the towers were built to accommodate them. The Menai tubular bridge was the largest rail bridge in the UK at that time, and had two main spans of 460 ft.

The spans of 1600 ft over the Forth proposed by Bouch were enormous, and it was natural that his first thought was to reduce the weight of his structure. This no doubt influenced him strongly towards the stiffened suspension bridge. He produced four designs on this principle, which are illustrated in Westhofen's book (Fig. 2.3).[4] Many suspension bridges of the day had a sag/span ratio for the chains of approximately 1:10, and three of Bouch's designs incorporated chains and stiffened chains of this form. The

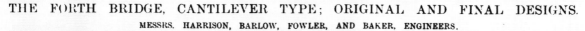

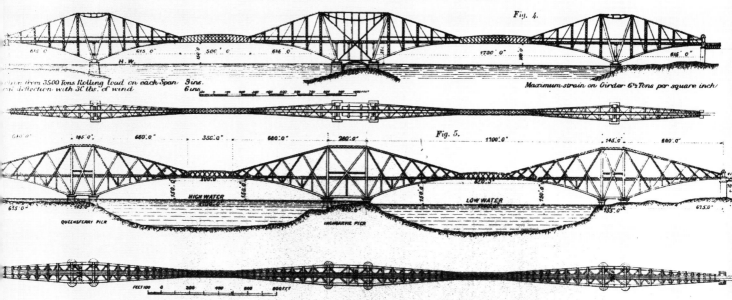

THE FORTH BRIDGE, CANTILEVER TYPE; ORIGINAL AND FINAL DESIGNS.
MESSRS. HARRISON, BARLOW, FOWLER, AND BAKER, ENGINEERS.

Fig. 2.5. The Forth Bridge: original and final designs by Fowler and Baker and others

fourth design, however, included chains with a sag/span ratio of about 1:4, which meant a sag of around 400 ft for the spans of 1600 ft. The clearance required for shipping was 150 ft, so that the towers required to support the chains and deck were nearly 600 ft in height, i.e. higher than the present road bridge towers (550 ft). This was the design favoured by Bouch, upon which construction had begun (Fig. 2.1).

Bouch evidently chose this low sag/span ratio to reduce the stresses in the chains, which were of steel and stressed to $10·0$ tons/in^2, high for those days (Fig. 2.3) (bottom). His three other designs had chains stressed to $8·0$ tons/in^2: as they had less sag, they must have had a greater area and weight of material to reduce the stress to this figure. For comparison, a maximum stress of $7·5$ tons/in^2 was adopted for the steel of the present Forth rail bridge, but only after prolonged negotiation with the Board of Trade by the engineers.

It is not clear why Bouch favoured this design, with its very large cable sag implying increased length of chains, height of towers, load on foundations, resistance to wind, and, of course, increased cost. Also, the large sag meant that the chains themselves were more prone to oscillation than chains with a shallower profile. The usual elegant curve of the chains generally lends suspension bridges an attractive appearance, but the large sag of the chains on Bouch's bridge made it look cumbersome. There were no suspended side

Fig. 2.6. Road bridge at Newcastle by Thomas Bouch, 1871

spans to match the 1600 ft main spans; this was also an awkward feature.

Distortion of the chains was to be precluded by tying them in position with radiating chain ties fixed to the ends of the stiffening girder. These ties were to assist the stiffening girder, which was 50 ft deep at mid-span, 18 ft deep at the ends, and of lattice construction. Also, the chains were anchored to the stiffening girders at their midpoints—an unusual feature.

Wind pressure for design purposes was assumed to be 10 lbs/ft^2, on the advice of the Astronomer Royal. This figure was also approved by Barlow and Pole in their report on Bouch's design in 1873, and seem to have been the norm for design in the UK at that time. Bouch separated the rail tracks in his bridge to two distinct structures 100 ft apart, bracing them to provide a rigid system against the horizontal forces of the wind. The chains for each of the two 1600 ft spans were anchored separately, so that the loading on one span did not affect the other. Temperature effects were also carefully assessed and suitable provision made.

The design seemingly gained Parliamentary and Board of Trade approval without any detailed investigation other than the private report by Barlow and Pole, and construction began in 1878, with William Arrol of Glasgow as Contractor. After the fall of the Tay Bridge in 1879 work was discontinued, and only the single foundation pier remains today (Fig. 2.4). Had Bouch's design been completed it might well have proved difficult and expensive to construct, owing to its multiplicity of small members. Barlow and Pole thought that it would require 'great accuracy in manufacture and erection'

Fig. 2.7. Cantilever 'Gerber' bridge at Hassfurt, Germany, 1869

and seemed to indicate a lingering doubt on its fitness for its purpose: 'While we raise no objection to Mr Bouch's system, we do not commit ourselves to an opinion that it is the best possible.' A modern day writer (Professor H. J. Hopkins) was more forthright and less kind when he commented that the design was 'painstakingly laboured to the point of being an oddity'.[5]

From time to time the question has been posed: 'would Bouch's Forth Bridge have stood up to gale force winds or succumbed as did the Tay?' The design was given a close examination by Barlow and Pole, and on the whole given a clean bill of health; however, it is clear from the description of the tall towers that their construction was to be of very much the same form as the piers that collapsed in the Tay. According to the 1873 Report:

> 'The height of the towers is 550 ft above the foundation tops. Each tower is formed of 8 hollow cast iron cylinders, varying from 3 to 4 ft in diameter with turned flanged joints strongly bolted together and connected with diagonal bracing or horizontal struts. . . .'

At the points where the chains passed over the tops of the towers they were not carried on rollers, but fixed to the tower tops. This would have meant that deformation of the chains through movement or loading or temperature would have produced flexure of the towers, albeit on a small scale. Barlow and Pole considered this acceptable.

However, such movement, however slight, could have had the effect of loosening the fixings of the bracing if the detail adopted had been the same as that in the Tay piers. Bearing in mind that the weakness of the bracing fixings was not apparent to Bouch until after the disaster, the bracing of the Forth Bridge towers might have been similar, and therefore weak.

The main horizontal load from the wind was applied to the Tay Bridge piers at their tops, where it had a maximum overturning effect. However, the load from the wind on the Forth Bridge towers operated at deck level, 150 ft above the water, i.e. at about a quarter of the towers' height. This meant that the towers had a greater measure of stability under wind loading than the Tay piers.

The report gives the stress in the cast iron towers as rather less than 4 tons/in^2, and states that the component of this stress due to wind was as low as ⅛ to ¼ ton/in^2. In these circumstances the wind force could have doubled or trebled without much effect on the cast iron towers; if so, provided the bracing was sound, the towers would have been safe. No details are given of the cross-section of the bracing itself or of the fixings—if they were designed as adequate only for 10 lbs/ft^2, to double or treble this load could have been disastrous.

The plan view of the horizontal bracing between the stiffening girders carrying the rail tracks shows it to be of single-triangular Warren type in form. The two tail tracks were 100 ft apart, therefore the struts in this arrangement would have been of the order of 140 ft long. These would have had to be of substantial construction to limit stresses and reduce deflection. A better arrangement would seem to have been the adoption of double-triangular bracing which Bouch was accustomed to using on his other bridges. This would have meant an additional weight of material, but would have reduced both the stresses in the struts and the deflection under wind. It is not known why Bouch adopted the Warren truss form for this particular bracing, especially given the magnitude of the dimensions—a horizontal truss 100 ft wide and 1600 ft long. It may be that he was being economical rather than practical. If this bracing was designed for 10 lbs/ft^2 and the wind loading doubled or trebled, the effect on the long slender struts might have been to produce buckling and a failure of the bracing.

In summary, the safety of Bouch's Forth Bridge would have been dependent on the adequacy of the bracing, both of the stiffening girder and of the towers. Perhaps the common sense and practical experience of Arrol, the Contractor, would have rescued the bridge from the danger of poor detailing, as happened many times in succeeding years, but if the bracing itself was inadequate then the fate of the bridge might have been very much in doubt.

In the past, bridges of two or four spans have been considered unattractive aesthetically because they formed an 'unresolved duality'. Bridges of three spans or five spans have been proposed for the sake of appearance. It can be seen that Bouch's design embodied an unresolved duality of awkward appearance in a way that the present bridge does not.

Fig. 2.8. Cantilever bridge over the Kentucky River, 1876

It is interesting that the calculations for Bouch's bridge, with its many degrees of redundancy, were exceedingly complex, and he was assisted by a Cambridge mathematician, Allan D. Stewart (see below and Chapter 5). When the bridge construction was abandoned, Stewart transferred his allegiance to Fowler and Baker, and became their chief assistant on the cantilever design. His name appears on the commemorative plaque on the present bridge.

Revised proposals by Fowler and Baker, 1881

After the Tay bridge disaster in 1879 the public and the press were loud in their criticism of Bouch's Forth Bridge design, and there was a massive loss of faith in the project. It soon became known that new and stringent regulations were to be introduced by the Board of Trade to control standards, and it was obvious that Bouch's design would have to be revised, particularly as it was designed for a wind pressure of only 10 lbs/ft^2.

The Railway Board formally abandoned Bouch's design on 13 January 1881 (i.e. a full year after the disaster), which indicates that they gave careful

Fig. 2.9. Articulation diagram for Kentucky River bridge

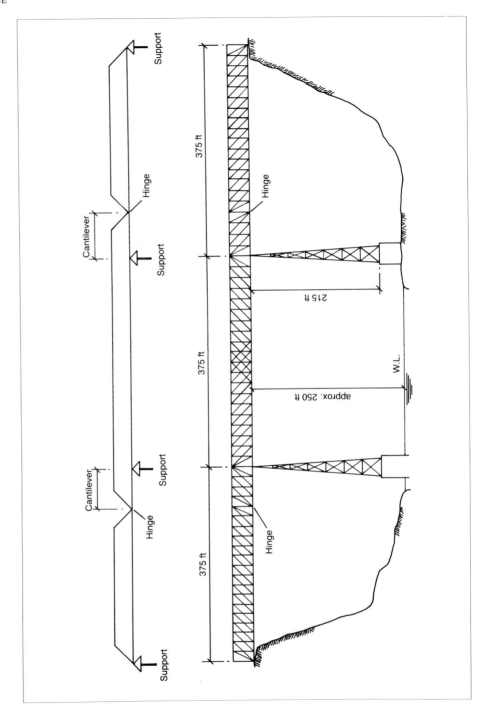

consideration to the matter. They cancelled the existing contracts and paid compensation where necessary. A formal Abandonment Bill was placed before Parliament, but a bridge, tunnel or some fixed means of communication across the Forth was still considered necessary, and the Abandonment Bill was withdrawn before it was passed.

New proposals for a bridge were invited from the Board's consulting engineers, Sir John Fowler, W. H. Barlow and T. E. Harrison. From these emerged a design proposal based on what was then called the 'continuous girder principle'. This entailed a continuous girder with definite breaks at chosen points of contraflexure. These breaks, or hinges, made the bridge form easier to calculate and build, and transformed it into a series of cantilevers and suspended spans rather than a continuous girder. This type of bridge had many advantages over the original stiffened suspension bridge, being more rigid and stable under construction. The original proposal was modified by Fowler and his junior partner, Benjamin Baker, to the form that we know today.

The original design had cantilever arms based on N-girder or Pratt truss panels with large 500 ft suspended spans in between (Fig. 2.5). The Fife and Queensferry cantilevers were not completely stable under construction until the landward arms had been completed. The revised design had a cantilever structure based on the double-triangular form, and shorter suspended spans of 350 ft. The Fife and Queensferry cantilevers were also designed to be selfsupporting at all stages of construction. This is the bridge we know today—the revised arrangement gave the impression of stability and strength.

These proposals gained the approval of the Board, and on 30 September 1881 Fowler and Baker were instructed to proceed with their design. A model 13 ft long was prepared specially for the House of Commons. (As late as 1955 this model was on public view at the Institution of Civil Engineers in London.) A new Bill passed through Parliament and received Royal Assent on 12 July 1882. Thus, within 18 months of the abandonment of Bouch's design a new bridge was well on the way.

Influenced by the widespread popular fears aroused by the Tay bridge failure, Parliament imposed many restrictions, including a new wind loading of 56 lbs/ft^2. It instructed the Board of Trade to inspect every stage of construction, no doubt mindful of the poor quality of ironwork inherent in the earlier disaster. The most important consideration was that the bridge 'should gain the confidence of the public, and enjoy a reputation of being not only the biggest and strongest, but also the stiffest bridge in the world'. By 'stiffness' they undoubtedly meant lack of noticeable movement or deflection under the passage of the trains or the violence of the winds.

In the 18 months of discussion between the abandonment of Bouch's design and the acceptance of Fowler and Baker's, the following criteria emerged as the basis of design of the bridge:

Fig. 2.10. Niagara Cantilever Bridge, 1883

(a) the maximum attainable rigidity, both vertically under the rolling load and laterally under wind pressure
(b) facility and security of erection, so that at any stage the incomplete structure would be as secure against a hurricane as the finished bridge
(c) that no untried material be used in the construction, and that no steel be used which did not comply with the requirements of the Admiralty, Lloyds and the Underwriters' Registry
(d) that the maximum economy be attained consistent with the fulfilment of the preceding conditions.

The proposed continuous girder bridge by Fowler and Baker complied more fully with these criteria than the previous stiffened suspension design.

Baker himself (on whom the main burden of design and supervision fell) had strong views on the requirements of a design, and as early as 1873 had stated in a lecture:

'Of all the numerous practical considerations and contingencies to be duly weighed and carefully estimated, before the fitness of a design for a longspan railway bridge can be satisfactorily determined, *none are more important* than those affecting facility of erection.'

From the above, it can be seen that the design of the Forth Bridge evolved in a particular form because of the simultaneous occurrence of a number of factors, each of low probability. These factors (and constraints) were

(a) the existence of a group of railway companies with the desire and the financial means to bridge the Forth

(b) the existence of the Queensferry site, with its high ground on either side allowing the necessary headroom, its wide deep-water channels precluding all but the largest spans, and the presence of rock and hard boulder clay offering suitable foundation material for a major bridge

(c) the availability of a new material, i.e. steel, of reliable quality, quantity and price

(d) the existence of engineers of the required towering vision, ability and courage to develop the design and bring about its realisation.

The present form of the bridge

The present form of the Forth Bridge is familiar to everyone, and we think of cantilever bridges of all types as being commonplace. But it was not always so. Before 1881, when Fowler and Baker put forward their proposals, the cantilever bridge was unknown in Britain; the designers of the new bridge were continually asked to justify it. This was important, as there would ultimately be no point in a bridge that did not inspire confidence in those who would be using it.

In particular, Baker was asked about his novel use of 'cantilevers'. He explained that the term means no more than 'bracket', and that an ordinary balcony or shelf is a form of cantilever. There was nothing novel even in the design of cantilever bridges; they had been built in China more than 200 years before, and probably earlier than that. There were also more recent examples of road and railway bridges in Europe and the USA built on the same principle, including a strange hybrid type of braced structure which Bouch had built across the Tyne at Newcastle in 1871 (Fig. 2.6).

As early as 1867, Benjamin Baker (then aged 27) had published a series of articles in *The Engineer* advocating the use of cantilevers supporting a girder system as the most effective means of providing bridges of long span. He and his senior partner Fowler had some experience of designing such bridges, for in 1864 they had proposed a bridge of 1000 ft span on the cantilever system for a railway crossing of the Severn. The span was subsequently reduced to 600 ft with 300 ft side-spans, and a contract was let for the works, which did not proceed due to financial problems. Again in 1871 they had prepared designs and estimates for a second proposal to cross the Severn in two spans of 800 ft each, but in this case also the design did not reach the construction stage. Fowler had taken part in a discussion on a Paper to the ICE as far back as 1850 on a continuous girder bridge at Torksey over the river Trent, which showed that even at that early stage, 30 years before the Forth bridge design, he had an accurate grasp of cantilever principles.

In addition to Fowler and Baker's designs, other engineers in Europe and the USA had produced at least three cantilever bridges before 1883.

(a) In 1866 the Bavarian engineer Heinrich Gerber was granted a patent for a design known as the 'Gerber girder', or in English speaking countries, a cantilever girder. This was a continuous girder over several spans in which hinged joints were inserted so that the harmful influence of minor settlement of supports was eliminated. The first bridge built by Gerber employing this system was in Germany over the river Main at Hassfurt in 1867. This had a central span of 426 ft (Fig. 2.7).

(b) In 1876 the Cincinnati Southern Railway crossed the Kentucky river by means of a cantilever bridge which had 3 equal spans of 375 ft. This was designed by an eminent American engineer, C. Shaler Smith (Figs 2.8 and 2.9).

(c) In 1883, the year work began at the Forth, a notable cantilever bridge was completed over the Niagara river in the USA by another leading American engineer, C. C. Schneider. This had a total length of 910 ft, was 239 ft above the water, and had a main span of 495 ft. It had pin-connected members, and was constructed in the amazingly short time of 10 months (Fig. 2.10).

There was also Bouch's bridge of 1871 at Newcastle (Fig. 2.6) which had main spans of 240 ft, braced with tension members from the tops of towers over the piers. These ties were fixed at the third points of the spans, and gave the bridge the appearance of a modern cablestayed structure or a cantilever bridge by Riccardo Morandi.

One of the basic questions affecting the form of the structure was the length of the cantilever arm in relation to the length of the suspended span. This was the subject of elaborate investigation by Baker, as it was known to have a pronounced effect on the economy of the design as well as on the method of erection. He chose lengths of 681·75 ft and 346·5 ft respectively (Fig. 2.11), giving a ratio of 1.96. But the first proposal by Fowler and Baker had a ratio of 1·23 due to the long suspended span of 500 ft (Fig. 2.4).

In the Quebec cantilever bridge of 1917 the ratio is 0·91, arising from a suspended span of 640 ft in a main span of 1800 ft (Fig. 2.12). This length of suspended span was so heavy that it had to be floated out and lifted into position, whereas Baker's smaller suspended spans could be constructed by cantilevering out from each side and joining up at mid-span. At Connel Ferry, Oban, completed in 1903, the ratio is even lower at 0·64 (Fig. 2.13). Thus, the Forth Bridge has rather short suspended spans compared to other designs of the period, but they look right.

Another feature of the bridge affecting its form was Baker's decision to have a small number of large, rather than a large number of small, structural members. Bouch's 1873 suspension bridge design illustrates the latter case. The towers and stiffening girders were of lattice construction, generating many connections and a probable substantial maintenance problem had it

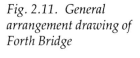

Fig. 2.11. General arrangement drawing of Forth Bridge

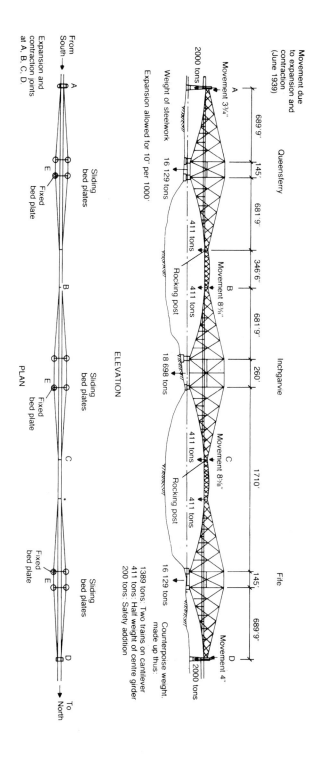

been built, owing to its multiplicity of members (Fig. 2.3). Baker's choice of few but large structural members was emphasised by his selection of tubes for the compression members of the bridge. These struts were up to 343 ft long and 12 ft in diameter, yet appear of slender proportions and even matchstick-like from a distance. (The vertical tubes over the piers have a length/breadth ratio of 28·6, as compared to 21·5 for a match) (Fig. 2.14).

Tubes were chosen because they are known to be the most efficient shape for a compression member, curved surfaces being much less prone to buckling than flat surfaces. Baker accepted that they would cost more to construct, but that this would be outweighed by the structural advantages. Nevertheless, the interpenetrations of the curved tubes at the skewbacks and elsewhere were extremely complex and difficult to design and detail as well as to construct.

Baker had to decide at an early stage how best to take the wind forces to the foundations, and he did this by introducing bracing between the tubular members, both in the webs and in the lower chords of the cantilever. The

Fig. 2.12. Quebec Bridge of 1917

QUEBEC BRIDGE
On the site of two disasters in bridge building, one a major one, stands this proud monument to perseverance in man

lattice girders in the upper chords and diagonals are unbraced. This arrangement led the wind forces to the piers by the shortest route; the tubular members were of course designed to accept this extra loading.

Careful provision was made for temperature movement (see Fig. 2.10). Also, Baker left three of the four skewbacks at the base of each cantilever tower free to move. Only one skewback in each group was fixed (Fig. 2.10). This was to allow the tremendous compression forces at the base of each cantilever arm to be resisted by the horizontal strut joining them. If this movement had not been allowed, the forces would have produced an overturning effect on the respective pier foundations.

Perhaps the most noticeable feature of the bridge, however, is the 'Holbein' straddle, i.e. the wide base of the cantilevers tapering to narrow widths both vertically and horizontally. The German artist, Hans Holbein, was wont to straddle the feet of male subjects in his pictures. Sir John Fowler knew this: when he met James Nasmith of steam-hammer fame by chance at a Holbein exhibition in London after the Tay bridge failure, he remarked that the bridge

Fig. 2.13. Connel Ferry Bridge, Oban, 1903

would not have fallen had it had a straddle to its piers resembling Holbein's characteristic pose. Hence the Holbein straddle, which resulted in a batter of about 1:7·5 throughout all the vertical members. This arrangement gave an impression of great stability, but also gave rise to much complexity in drawing and detailing, and in construction (Fig. 2.16).

Materials and allowable stresses

In the late 1870s when the Forth Bridge was being designed, steel remained a comparatively untried material for bridges, although it had been employed since the 1850s in several ships, including the 'Columba', the most famous of all the Clyde steamers, which was built in 1878 and queened it on the Clyde for more than 50 years. Steel was considered a new material, and some engineers had reservations about its brittleness as compared to that of wrought iron. It was also impossible to define its character completely by chemistry and ingredients, and testing of specimens was necessary to obtain sufficient proof of its quality and strength.

In the rebuilding of the Tay bridge conservatism held sway, and wrought iron was used. Corresponding maximum stresses of 5·0 ton/in^2 in tension and 4·80 tons/in^2 in compression were adopted. However, steel could offer a 50% increase on these working stresses, and was obviously a great attraction where long spans were concerned, since its weight differed little from that of wrought iron. Fowler and Baker therefore approached the Board of Trade to find out the maximum stress which could be adopted in design. At that time the Board was allowing 6·5 tons/in^2, but Baker showed that by improving the quality of the steel, 7·5 tons/in^2, i.e. a quarter of the ultimate strength of the steel would be reasonable, and the Board accepted this figure. Its figure of 6·5 tons/in^2 had been based on steel with an ultimate strength of 26 tons/in^2, whereas Baker proposed a minimum of 30 tons/in^2 for the bridge. Nowadays, BS 449 would allow a working stress in tension of 10·6 tons/in^2 on a steel of this ultimate stress.

Baker was aware of the dangers of fatigue, and limited the stress in the wind bracing, which was subject to alternate tension and compression, to 5·0 tons/in^2. Elsewhere on the bridge the working stress was to be 3·33 tons/in^2 if the stresses alternated in this fashion. He recognised that in the case of a hurricane the repetitions of stress would be few and far between, and so allowed a higher stress (Fig. 2.15).

The Board of Trade regulations for the use of steel in the bridge were minimal, simply stating that the working stress should not exceed 25% of the ultimate. No distinction was made between tensile and compressive stress, or between stresses produced by dead and live load, either alone or in combination. Fowler and Baker therefore derived their design rules for stresses by careful thought and experiment, and their caution and insight has been amply repaid in the 100 year life of the bridge so far. Fatigue has not been a problem in the main structure, but has necessitated some repairs to the

*Fig. 2.14. Inchgarvie
Tower, Forth Bridge*

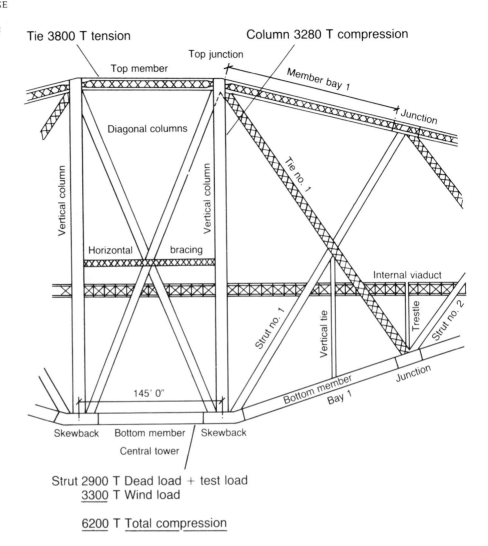

Fig. 2.15. Baker's figures for forces in members

Tie 3800 T tension

Column 3280 T compression

Top junction

Top member

Member bay 1

Junction

Diagonal columns

Vertical column

Tie no. 1

Vertical column

Horizontal   bracing

Internal viaduct

Strut no. 1

Vertical tie

Trestle

Strut no. 2

145′ 0″

Bottom member
Bay 1

Junction

Skewback   Bottom member / Skewback

Central tower

Strut 2900 T Dead load + test load
       <u>3300</u> T Wind load

       <u>6200</u> T <u>Total compression</u>

internal viaduct. In the latter, of course, live load plays a much greater part than dead load, although in the main structure the reverse applies.

In the construction of the tubes and other members, Baker insisted that as far as possible all plates and bars were to be bent cold. Where heating was essential, no work was to be done on the material after it had fallen to a 'blue' heat. He also insisted that the steady pressure of hydraulic riveting was to be used in place of hammering wherever possible, and that annealing would be required if the steel had been overworked in any way. He allowed no punching of holes or shearing of edges, and specified that all plates were to be planed at the edges, and all holes drilled. In particular, holes were to be drilled through multiple thicknesses of plates and angles after assembly.

These recommendations show the care with which Baker considered his material and its interconnection. Nothing was left to chance; painstaking attention to detail prevailed throughout. Having chosen the quality of steel and the working stresses, Baker then designed his structure boldly and confidently to the set limits.[6–8]

Incidentally, the Author has not been able to locate any mention of Baker employing extra material or thickness to allow for the effects of corrosion in such an exposed location. In the event, his confidence in the effective maintenance of the bridge was not misplaced; it has been exceedingly well painted and maintained over the last 100 years.

Analysis—forces in the struts and ties

None of Baker's published papers give any hint of the methods used in calculating the structure. His book '*Long span railway bridges*', published in 1873, does not go into structural analysis or stress calculation; it outlines general principles. Recourse to the Mitchell Library in Glasgow, where some of the original Arrol drawings are stored, indicated that no calculations have been filed. It has therefore not been possible to locate any relevant calculations, but the method of calculation is known.

As mentioned above, Baker was assisted in his calculations by a Cambridge mathematician named Allan D. Stewart, who had earlier assisted Bouch in his calculations for the stiffened suspension bridge. For this rather more complex bridge Stewart is known to have used what he called 'diagrams of forces' evolved by Professor Clerk Maxwell (1831–1879), a well-known physicist of the 19th century, of course, whose work embraced many fields. Clerk Maxwell evolved the load displacement method and reciprocal theorems in 1864 for analysing structures.

Allan Stewart presented a Paper to the ICE in 1892[9] on 'Stresses and deflections in braced girders'. In those days the words 'stress' and 'strain' were commonly used where 'force' is the equivalent term today, and the paper is actually about forces and deflections. In it, Stewart shows how a method of calculation which he calls 'the principle of elastic forces' can be applied to double triangular girders and other redundant structures with great accuracy, and states that this method was used in the calculation of the Forth bridge structure. He also gives an example of its use for calculation of deflection at the counterweighted shore arms of the Fife and Queensferry cantilevers. Stewart's name appears on the plaque on the bridge as Fowler and Baker's chief assistant, and there seems little doubt that he was responsible for the basic calculations for the Forth Bridge.

It will be noted that the bridge is almost entirely composed of girders of the double triangular arrangement of an even number of panels in each span, i.e. the approach girders, the central suspended spans, and the cantilever arms.

This form of truss, if the upper and lower chords are straight, is calculated approximately by separating the double triangular system into two single systems, each loaded with 50% of the total load, then superimposing the two results for the total forces in the members. Textbooks of the period claim that this method gives accuracy to within 5% of a more rigorous redundant structure analysis such as Allan Stewart's method. When the upper or lower chord of the girder is curved, however, it is more difficult to apply because of the resulting 'kinks' in the members of the single systems, and a more detailed method of analysis is required.

In calculating the wind effects, Baker assumed the circular form of the tubes to give a reduction in resistance of 50% as compared to a flat surface. He also took the wind force on the leeward structure as being equal to that on the windward structure; an assumption on the safe side. The assumption regarding the streamlining effect of the tubular surface is almost exactly that quoted in CP3 today.

In the cantilevers Baker gave figures of 3300 tons for the dead load and train test load, and 2900 tons for the wind force in the central lower chord strut, giving a total of 6200 tons. The net area of this strut is 830 in^2, giving a stress of 7·47 tons/in^2. The strut has a slenderness ratio of about 29, being 12 ft in diameter with 1¼ inch plating and 145 ft long, but restrained by some fixity at the ends. The allowable total stress was 7·5 tons/in^2, lower than would be allowed today, and no additional 25% increase was allowed for wind loading (Fig. 2.15).

The greatest load on a lattice girder tie member in the top chord is approximately 3800 tons. No wind load was taken on these members, which makes the calculation rather easier. The area in tension is 506 in^2, giving a tensile stress of 7·50 tons/in^2. The vertical column over the skewback is 343 ft high, 12 ft in diameter and the shell is of plating ⅝ inch thick. The area in compression is about 468 in^2, and Baker gives a force of 3280 tons in the strut, i.e. about 7·0 tons/in^2. The strut has a slenderness ratio of about 34, being braced at mid-height. The slenderness ratio is thus higher than the central lower chord strut, which may account for the slightly lower stress shown in the calculation. Baker states in his paper to the British Association that no attempt was made to calculate temperature effects in the bridge members, although of course ample provision for temperature movement was made in the bridge as a whole.

The method of using influence lines for forces in members, widely used in railway bridge work, was derived in Germany by Weyrauch as early as 1873 and first appeared in the English language in 1887 in a paper to the American Society of Engineers. Its use was slow to develop in this country, and it is unlikely that influence lines were used in the calculation of any of the members of the Forth Bridge. They would have been of little use in the calculation of forces in the cantilevers, but might have had some application

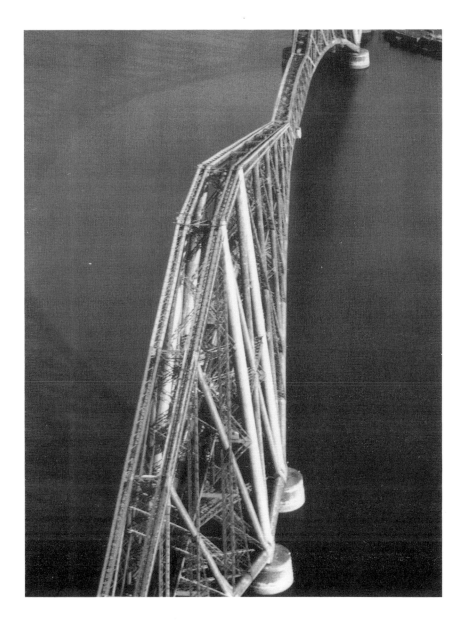

Fig. 2.16. Inclined structure of Forth Bridge: the Holbein straddle

in the girders of the approach spans, or in the decking and the internal viaduct.

The magnitude of the structure and the forces deriving from it takes it beyond the range of simple modes of calculation which are customary in structures of a more ordinary kind. Influences which are usually small and

Fig. 2.17. The Gossamer Bridge—delicate and graceful

can be handled easily have in this case to be carefully studied, particularly the dead load of the tubes and other members spanning between the panels, stiffness of the joints, torsion effects in the cantilevers due to trains on one line only, and the effects of the wind bracing on the tubes where the bracing does not reach a base reaction point. The locked-in stresses due to erection procedures would add to these problems, as would temperature effects of many kinds including sunshine on one side only of the bridge.

Baker forecast that the heaviest train traversing the bridge would not deflect the 1700 ft span more than 4 inches. In this he was remarkably accurate, as a deflection of 3½ inches has actually been measured on the bridge. He also calculated that a wind pressure equivalent to 30 lbs/ft^2 over the entire 1700 ft span would bend the bridge laterally less than 9 inches. He did not give a figure for a pressure of 56 lbs/ft^2, perhaps because it was unlikely that such a pressure would ever act over the whole structure.

It is interesting that Baker in his public lectures up to the year 1885 gave the estimate for the weight of steel in the cantilever structures of the bridge as totalling 42 000 tons, excluding the approach viaducts. In a lecture in 1887 he gave the figure as 45 000 tons, after erection of the steelwork had begun. However, the final figure given by Westhofen is 51 000 tons, 21% higher than the original estimate.

Westhofen speaks of alterations to the design and the increase of cross-section in various parts. The extra steel may have been necessary because of the weights of the cranes and other plant on individual members during erection, where cantilevering out over long lengths took place. The internal stiffening to the great tubes may not have been refined in detail, and perhaps the internal viaduct was not fully designed at the estimating stage. Other complex interpenetrations of tubes such as the 12 skewbacks are unlikely to have been fully detailed at that stage either, and may have required more steel than allowed for. There are many reasons why the original estimate may have been low, but if Baker used a figure of 42 000 tons in his calculations, he must have designed with a good margin in hand to allow for an increase in dead load of 21% for the cantilever structure of the bridge. Digesting these figures has been a fascinating exercise, but suggests that the Forth bridge is not so over-designed as is often supposed!

Most views of the bridge are from the shore close by, where foreshortening gives it a heavy appearance. Seen from the road bridge, however, the railway bridge is slender and graceful, leaping like a greyhound over the vast span of

Fig. 2.18. The completed Forth Bridge

water between the cantilevers. In spite of the constraints of high wind loads and low steel stresses, Baker achieved a graceful and elegant design (Figs. 2.17 and 2.18).

Subsequent cantilever bridge designs

In completing this review of the design of the Forth Bridge, it may be useful to compare other cantilever bridges of the same period.

Lansdowne Bridge, India, 1889

This bridge was designed by A. M. Rendel for railway traffic over the Indus at Sukkur. It was completed in 1889, and for 10 months, until the completion of the Forth Bridge in 1890, held the record for the world's largest cantilever span (Fig. 2.19). It had a span of 810 ft, less than half the spans at Queensferry, but almost twice that of the biggest UK rail bridge up to that time. Some years ago it was correctly written that 'in this structure the lamp of truth shines with too lurid a flame'. It was a rather unattractive structure, which was almost completely pre-erected in Britain before being dismantled, transported to the site and re-erected.

Like the Forth, the Lansdowne Bridge had the Holbein straddle for stability. Instead of tubes for compression members, it employed curious built-up lattice members reminiscent of the jib of a derrick crane. Again we see the Victorian love of multiplicity of small members. The bridge has been dismantled and no longer exists.

Connel Ferry Bridge, 1903

This bridge crosses the Falls of Lora at the entrance to Loch Etive, Argyll. It was located on a minor branch railway line, the Oban to Ballachulish railway, and completed in 1903 (Fig. 2.13).

Fig. 2.19. Lansdowne Bridge over the River Indus, India, 1889

The main span is 525 ft with a 232 ft suspended span. The bridge has a rather curious outer tapering support structure and an inner suspended structure which in reality comprises the whole of the bridge. Again it has a straddle for stability. The tubes in compression are rectangular and square, with stiffening on the outside, rather like the bodywork seams on a Mini car.

It can be seen that the shore arms of the cantilevers are short, and the bridge would tip up were it not counterweighted at the abutment. The contractor, as for the Forth Bridge, was Sir William Arrol & Co. It is still in use as a road bridge, the branchline having closed in 1962.

The Quebec Bridges of 1907 and 1917

The first cantilever bridge planned over the St. Lawrence river at Quebec had a span of 1800 ft, some 90 ft greater than the Forth Bridge spans of 20 years before. It was well on the way to completion in 1907 when it was the scene of a disaster equalling that of the Tay. One of the almost completed cantilevers collapsed with the loss of 75 lives. The reasons for the disaster are beyond the scope of this review, but one contributory factor was that the designer had increased the span from 1600 to 1800 ft late in the design stage, and did not recalculate the dead load, which led to overstressing of the structural members.

Much of the bridge was composed of tension members of eyebar links, and slender struts of plated side walls connected by lacing battens. The designer, Theodore Cooper, had previously criticised the Forth Bridge for being over-designed and expensive—after his Quebec bridge fell, someone was unkind enough to write to the engineering press and quote him. The bridge was rebuilt in 1917 and completed after another serious accident which cost 11 lives. It has box struts and a lack of straddle, but is a convincing design none the less (Fig. 2.12).

Conclusion

This necessarily brief review of the origins and design of the Forth Bridge has tried to show something of the thinking behind it, and the boldness, original thought and painstaking care which went into its design. It is a beautiful bridge, second to none in the world, and our country is the richer because of it. Long may it survive to inspire others with its majesty and grace!

Acknowledgements

The Author is indebted to the staff of ScotRail for assistance in visiting the bridge and in preparing this Paper, in particular to Mr W. D. F. Grant, Area Civil Engineer, Scotland South-East. He is also indebted to Mr Roland Paxton, Chairman of the ICE Panel for Historical Engineering Works, without whose assistance and encouragement the Paper would never have been written. The photographs in Figs 2.14, 2.15 and 2.18 were prepared from slides kindly supplied by Patricia Macdonald, photographer.

References

1. Harris A. J. Civil Engineering considered as an art. *Proc. Instn. Civ. Engrs*, Part I, 1975, **58**, 15–23
2. *The aims of structural design*. The Institution of Structural Engineers, 1969.
3. Barlow W. H. and Pole W. *Report on the Forth Bridge designed by Thomas Bouch*. 1873.
4. Westhofen W. *The Forth Bridge*. London, 1890.
5. Hopkins H. J. *A span of bridges*. David and Charles, 1970.
6. Baker R. The Forth Bridge. *J. Iron Steel Inst.*, No. 11, 1885.
7. Baker B. *The Forth Bridge*. Lecture to the British Association, 1882.
8. Baker B. *Bridging the Firth of Forth*. Lecture to the Royal Institution, 1887.
9. Stewart A. D. Stresses and deflections in braced girders. *Proc. Instn Civ. Engrs*, 1892.

CHAPTER 3

Construction of the bridge

W. R. Cox, *Sir William Arrol – NEI Thompson Ltd*

The construction of the Forth Bridge represented a major step forward in the fabrication and erection of large steel structures, and introduced techniques and systems which are still used in principle today. The bridge was designed and built against a background of tragedy and doubt engendered by the failure of the first Tay Bridge, designed by Sir Thomas Bouch, in December 1879. About 1000 yards of bridge collapsed during a gale, taking with it a train and its passengers. Some 20 lives had been lost during construction, and 75 in the disaster. Bouch, who was severely criticised at the public enquiry, had also designed a suspension bridge to cross the River Forth but this plan was subsequently rejected.

It was decided to build a new Tay Bridge some 60 ft clear of the old structure to a design by W. H. Barlow. The contract for this bridge was let to William Arrol of Glasgow, who began work in 1882 and completed it in 1887.

Contract for the Forth Bridge

The Bill for undertaking the bridge was passed by a special committee of the House of Commons on 19 May 1882, following an 8 day enquiry. No 'opposition of substance' to the design was raised, indeed some navigational opposition was thought to have been fostered by opposing railway interests.

An important point arose during the enquiry preceding the passage of the Bill. For the first time, an attempt was made by a Parliamentary Committee to appoint an authority to exercise control and supervision over the responsible engineers. However, the engineers associated with the Forth Bridge had sufficient influence to induce the Board of Trade to join them in pointing out to the Committee the '. . . infinite mischief which must inevitably result if the responsible engineers of an undertaking were subject to the control of an outsider, however judicious or eminent.' In the event, the then President of the Board of Trade, Mr Chamberlain, withdrew the suggested clause referring to outside inspection. However, it was agreed that Major General Hutchinson, on behalf of the board, should inspect and report on the works every 3 months during progress.

On 21 December 1882, the contract for the construction of the bridge was let

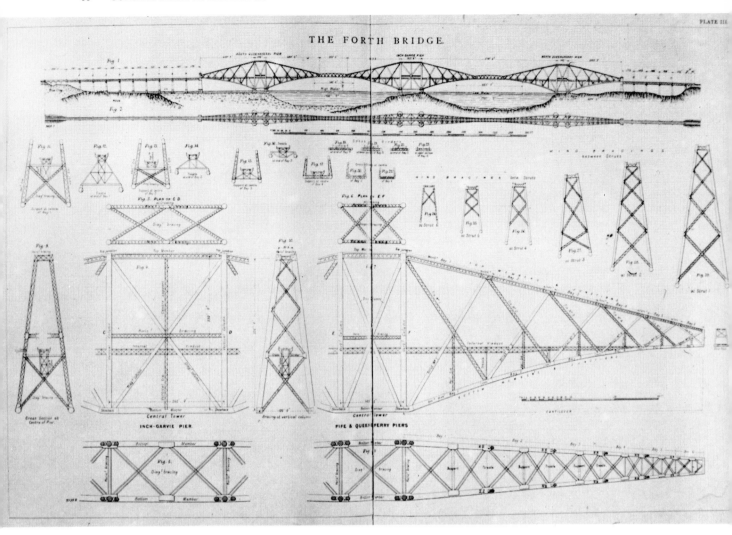

Fig. 3.1. General arrangement of the superstructure

to Sir Thomas Tancred, Mr T. H. Falkiner and Mr Joseph Phillips, civil engineers and contractors of Westminster; and Messrs Arrol & Co. of the Dalmarnock Ironworks, Glasgow. The contract sum was £1 600 000; tenders ranged from £1 487 000 to £2 301 000.

As this Chapter deals with construction, a few words on William Arrol, the Contractor, might be appropriate. Born in Renfrewshire in 1839, Arrol was a self-made man, having been apprenticed as a blacksmith at the age of 13 and then worked in England. Returning to Scotland, he worked as a blacksmith, fitter and boiler maker, becoming foreman of the bridge and boiler departments of Laidlaw & Sons, Glasgow and Edinburgh. About 1872, he set up on his own with a capital of £250 and obtained contracts for a number of iron bridges including those on the Glasgow, Hamilton and Bothwell Railway. This work was followed by two bridges over the Clyde adjoining Glasgow Central Station, for which he designed a number of special machines for drilling and a riveting machine driven by hydraulics. With work on the massive new Tay Bridge in hand, confidence was expressed that William Arrol could safely be entrusted with the construction of the Forth Bridge. This

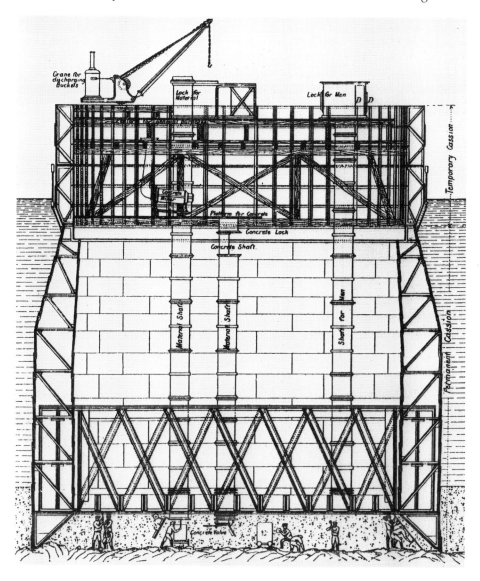

Fig. 3.2. Section of pneumatic caisson

confidence, in the event, proved more than justified—100 years later. However, having been in business for a little over 10 years, it is unlikely that he would have cleared such hurdles as vendor assessment, pre-tender questionnaire, quality audit to BS 5750, etc.

Sir Thomas Tancred, who was associated with Arrol when the contract was let, was a professional engineer with experience in other countries, including New Zealand. He later left the partnership and William Arrol became sole structural fabricator and erector.

The main structural towers are referred to as Queensferry (South), Inchgarvie (Central) and Fife (North). These three towers, each with its huge cantilevers, two suspended spans and approach viaduct steel spans, ten on the south and five on the north, together with four short masonry arches on

Fig. 3.3. Caisson under construction at South Queensferry

the south and three on the north, complete the bridge. (Fig. 3.1).

The total length of the main bridge structure is 5349 ft 6 inches, with around 1980 ft of viaduct on the south and 970 on the north, over 1½ miles in total. The level of the twin track railway is 157 ft above high water. The clear headway under the centre of the bridge is 150 ft, and the highest part of the bridge 361 ft above high water. The piers contain some 120 000 cubic yards of concrete and masonry, and the superstructure comprises some 50 000 tons of steel connected by around 6 500 000 rivets.

The use of cast iron on the ill-fated Tay Bridge had been deemed a factor in its failure, so for the Forth Bridge it was determined to use steel with closely controlled properties. For areas in tension, the steel had a tensile strength of 30/33 tons/in^2, with 20% minimum elongation; for areas in compression,

Fig. 3.4. Top portion of foundation under construction within temporary caisson

material of 34/37 tons/in^2 with elongation of 17% minimum was used (see Fig. 2.15, p. 58). Regular checks were made on the steel quality—the approval for the works stipulated that they should be inspected every 3 months by General Hutchinson or other inspecting officers of the Board of Trade. The steel came from Landore in Wales (12 000 tons) and Steel Co. of Scotland in Newton and Blochairn (46 000 tons).

The work

Work fell into four categories, some concurrent and some consecutive:

(a) site preparation
(b) foundations and masonry piers
(c) prefabrication of steel
(d) erection of steel in main spans and approaches.

Fig. 3.5. Inchgarvie foundation showing granite facing and holding down bolts

The contract was let on 21 December 1882; the bridge was opened to traffic on 4 March 1890. Key dates in the construction were:

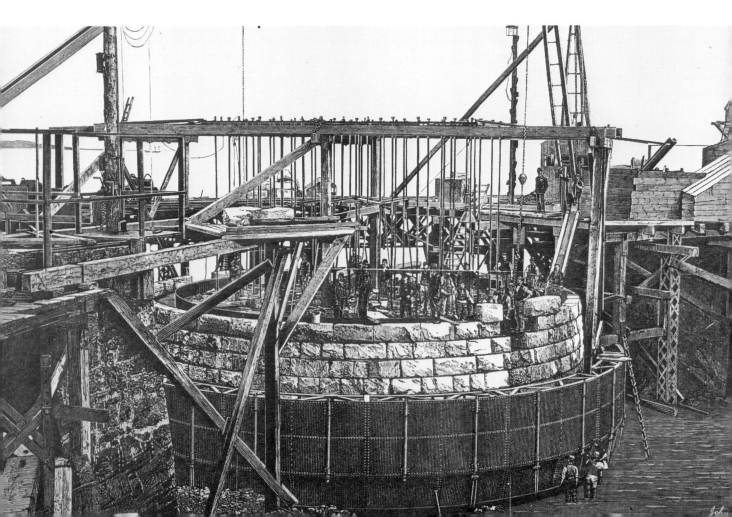

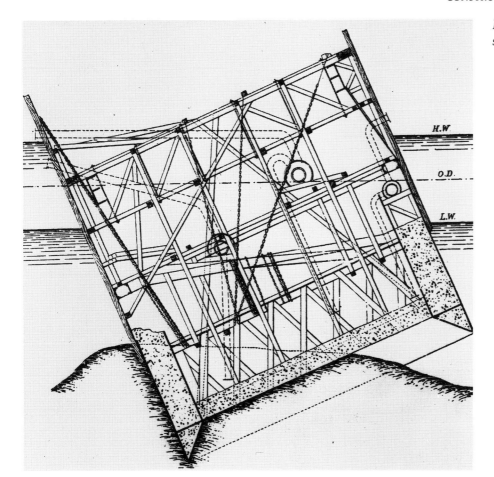

Fig. 3.6. Section of tilted south Queensferry caisson

Contract let	21 December	1882
Completion of south jetty	May	1884
Launching of sixth and last caisson	May	1885
Raising of viaduct piers and girders	July	1887
Completion of 12 main pier foundations	June	1886
Start of steel tower erection	June	1886
Completion of 3 main steel towers	Mid	1887
Completion of all 6 cantilevers	July	1889
Completion of suspended spans	November	1889
Test load by trains	January	1890
Official opening of bridge	4 March	1890

Foundations and piers

The first task was to establish the position for the bridge extremely accurately. A base line about 4000 ft long was established along the high ground on the southern shore of the Firth, commencing on the centre line of the bridge near the southernmost end of the Queensferry viaduct and extending eastwards to a point near the North British railway line, about 4000 ft away. Also, an observatory was set up at the outer end of a stone jetty near Port Edgar, about 1300 ft into the Firth, and 20 setting-out points were created to form the basis of a triangulation.

The setting-out work on the bridge was conducted by a Mr Reginald Middleton, some of whose comments are interesting to note. After carrying out an initial survey by triangulation and in some instances by direct measurement, he concluded that a better result would have been obtained if he had trusted entirely to triangulation, and that 'In such a situation, a direct measurement is not to be relied on.'

Mr Middleton also commented that

'Benchmarks cut in stone or wood are not to be relied on. For very accurate work, it is better in the case of stone or concrete to insert a copper bolt and mark down with a centre punch and for marks on timber a copper tack scored across with a knife gives the same result. A broad arrow may be cut in alongside to call attention to the mark if necessary.'

On the subject of surveying poles he noted that

'Fixed poles should be of the same diameter throughout and securely fixed plumb and must be at the same time easily movable. If they are not made of one diameter, it is possible that some part of the pole may be out of centre. The writer has found white poles with three or four black rings painted on them, each ring being some 2 inches deep, the best for sighting in. If there had been a larger amount of black, they will become dim and are not easily distinguished.'

The theodolites used were 12 inch transit made by Messrs Cooke & Sons of York, divided to 10 seconds and fitted with a central plug for supporting the plumb bob which, when removed, gave place to a centring telescope fitted with cross hairs by means of which the instrument could be centred without the use of the bob. Mr Middleton suggested this arrangement to the makers, and found it to be of the greatest value, as he could be quite certain of its accurate setting in all weathers.

At Inchgarvie, an exposed island, and at North Queensferry stores and offices were built and iron staging for the pierwork was constructed and pinned to the rock. By October 1884 a very large quantity of plant had been assembled on site, including 14 steam barges, launches and other vessels; 2 steam, 12 hydraulic and 38 hand power cranes; 28 single and double engines

Fig. 3.7. *View of tilted caisson at South Queensferry pier*

for shop machines, hydraulic work, air compressors, electric lighting, pumping etc.; gas furnaces for heating the steel plates, a 2000 ton press for bending them, and planing machines, multiple drills, hydraulic riveters and other special machines. The initial site work involved the construction of the support piers. No special difficulty arose with the southern viaduct piers, which were executed either in tidal conditions or in half tide or full tide cofferdams.

The cofferdam for the Queensferry cantilever support tower was a massive affair—126 by 75 ft overall, with a double row of timber piles with 4 ft of puddle clay between them, together with raking struts. Satisfactory conditions were found at varying depths down to 38 ft below high water. The piers were faced with Aberdeen granite 2 ft thick, backed with concrete and rubble masonry. About every 12 ft a layer of large stones was laid across the piers. The North Queensferry approach piers proved more difficult, as the rock was on quite a severe slope which had to be levelled by diamond drilling and blasting.

Fig. 3.8. *Skewback and main column showing arrangement of curved plating*

Fig. 3.9. Hydraulic press for bending plates

Each of the three main towers is supported by four separate foundations, which were constructed within iron caissons 70 ft in diameter. The four foundations at the Queensferry pier, being founded on boulder clay, were sunk under compressed air. The four foundations for the Fife main pier were constructed in open caissons as they were landed on rock. The two southern foundations on the Inchgarvie pier were also sunk under compressed air conditions, but its two northern foundations were founded on rock and were sunk in open conditions.

For the lower portion of the Queensferry piers, four steel pneumatic caissons were built on shore, floated out and lowered into position. (Figs 3.2 and 3.3). These piers, 70 ft in diameter at the cutting edge, with a 1 in 46 taper to facilitate sinking, were sunk under compressed air to depths of 68–88 ft below high water. They had an internal skin 7 ft from the outer skin; this formed pockets which were loaded with stone or concrete to ensure that the caisson had sufficient weight to move down vertically. The compressed air locks were of a new design by William Arrol and Benjamin Baker.

The last of the six pneumatic caissons required at Inchgarvie's two south

Fig. 3.10. (above) Trial
assembly of main column
at South Queensferry yard

Fig. 3.11. (right) General
view of assembly yard,
South Queensferry

piers was floated out with due ceremony on 29 May 1885, when Lord and Lady Aberdeen went to South Queensferry by train. Lady Aberdeen operated the lever of the hydraulic machinery to the cheers of a large crowd.

Below low water each caisson was filled with concrete, leaving a 7 ft working space under compressed air (Fig. 3.2). The sinking of the pneumatic caissons was placed as a subcontract with M. Coiseau of Paris and Antwerp, and the work was undertaken mainly by Italian, Belgian, Austrian and German labour. Above the caissons the piers were built in very strong masonry, 55 ft in diameter at the bottom, 49 ft at the top, and 36 ft high (Fig. 3.4). At the top of each cylindrical pier 48 steel bolts of 2½ inch diameter and 24 ft long were cast to hold down the bed plates of the steel structure (Fig. 3.5).

The only major unforeseen delay on the contract arose from the accidental tilting of one of the caissons, at the north-west of the Queensferry pier (Figs 3.6 and 3.7). Due to a combination of very high and low spring tides, this sank unevenly into the mud and then slid some 20 ft, so that the top, to which divers then had to fasten strengthening plates, was about 6 ft under water at low tide. During pumping out, the external water pressure caused some of

Fig. 3.12. North approach viaduct during construction

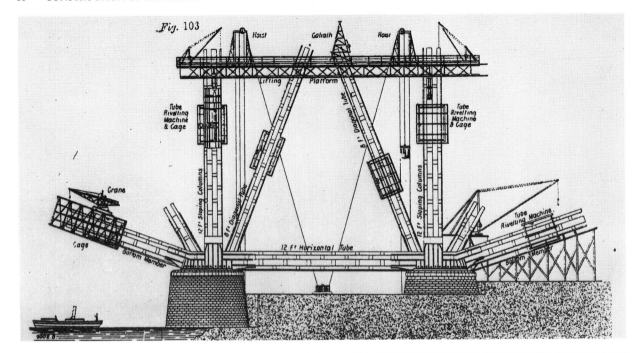

Fig. 3.13. (above)
Schematic diagram of
main tower erection
equipment

Fig. 3.14. View of tower
erection in progress

*Fig. 3.15. Fife main
tower completed*

the plates to tear, and the caisson had to be substantially stiffened with timber before it could be righted. The delay was of about 10 months on this pier.

Fabrication of the structure

The vast bulk of the fabrication was carried out in specially built shops and level yard areas adjacent to the bridge site at South Queensferry. An area of 20 acres was laid out for the construction of the steelwork, connected directly to the North British Railway and by an incline and winding engine to a temporary timber viaduct. This extended to the four main foundations for the Queensferry tower.

Fig. 3.16. Schematic diagram of cantilever erection equipment

William Arrol was faced with the massive task of producing very large quantities of large diameter tubes, which formed all the main compression members of the bridge. The limited size of plate available meant that these tubes (mostly 12 ft in diameter) had to be made up from a number of curved plates with stiffened longitudinal joints. Each tube length of some 16 ft had a circumferential joint with a stiffener ring at 8 ft centres (Fig. 3.8). All the joints had to be drilled and riveted.

Accuracy was important, as were time and cost. A number of trials on bending the plates cold were made—these plates were up to 1¼ inches thick, and achieving final accuracy was difficult. Alarm was also raised when some plates cracked in a brittle manner from the sheared edges—this phenomenon is still a problem today. It was decided that the effects of shearing should be

Fig. 3.17. Lower boom erection

Fig. 3.18. Cantilever erection

eliminated by planing after the plates had been bent hot; a final adjustment was made by repressing when they were cold. For this work a special gas plate heating furnace was built, and a hydraulic bending press set up nearby (Fig. 3.9).

Following the bending, the plates were formed into tubes around a mandrel and the holes were drilled through plates, covers and bars in a single operation (Fig. 3.10). Four specially designed annular drilling frames surrounding the tubes, each fitted with ten drills, were built for this purpose, running along rails so that every hole required could be drilled and of length such that four 400 ft lengths of tube could be drilled at one time (Fig. 3.11). In a 16 ft length of 12 ft diameter tube there were some 1600 holes to drill through thicknesses of 2¼–3¼ inches of steel. Such work took about 52 hours.

The junction of the main horizontal 12 ft diameter tubes and the vertical tubes, together with the connection to the pier bases, was a matter for very careful consideration, and part sized timber mock ups were built from which the eventual shapes were determined. Such a joint must connect eight intersecting members, five tubular and three lattice, and was called a 'skewback'. Several layers of plates formed the 'upper bed-plate'; the 'lower bed-plate' was also formed from several layers of plates riveted together on site by a specially designed machine and bolted down to the pier top. This system was designed to allow a limited amount of sliding between the structure and the pier, movement being controlled by a large dowel. At each main pier only one of the four columns is fixed positively to the foundation.

The tension members and cross bracings were generally of box lattice construction, drilled by similar machines to those used for the tubes.

Bridge erection

The viaducts comprising ten spans at the south end and five at the north were the first sections erected. These were initially erected at low level over their piers, and then raised by a series of jacking operations followed by the raising of the masonry in the pier as required (Fig. 3.12).

On the main towers, the first work was the installation and riveting of the lower bed-plates. These were riveted by a special machine, and were 37 ft by 17 ft 8 inches by 3–4 inches thick.

After completion and lowering, the upper bed-plates were similarly constructed, and to them were attached the various connections for the main steelwork of the skewbacks. Parts of this structure were complex and required work in confined spaces. Special small hydraulic riveting machines were constructed operating at pressures as high as 3 tons/in^2.

Steam derrick cranes were erected on platforms some 30–40 ft above deck level and commanding the whole of the skewbacks. These were built with portions of the diagonal struts, the vertical columns and the cantilever struts to as great a height as could be reached. This work was conducted with extreme care, and the joints were only bolted up after the necessary checks and corrections had been made by means of theodolites. The setting out of the work was difficult: the members not only had to be set with an inclination towards the next point of intersection, but also had to follow the uniform batter of the vertical columns—there was therefore a strong tendency for the members to lean towards the centre of the towers. As soon as the vertical columns and struts had been built to a height of about 50 ft above deck, preparations were made for the construction of the lifting platforms by means of which the central towers would be raised to their full height (Fig. 3.13). A staging reaching out to the north and south from column to column and about 25 ft in width was raised from the deck to a height of about 30 ft above the level of the pier, and on this a pair of longitudinal girders were built. These girders were about 190 ft long in the case of the Fife and the Queensferry towers, and 350 ft for the much larger Inchgarvie tower. There were four girders, one to each side of the vertical columns, placed 18½ ft apart with angle cross bracings.

The main booms and most of the vertical angle bracing were in fact part of the permanent work, the booms being portions of the ties in the cantilevers

Fig. 3.19. (facing page, top) General view of construction: summer 1888

Fig. 3.20. (facing page, bottom) Queensferry main cantilevers during construction

borrowed for this purpose. Using an intricate and ingenious system of movable support girders, the platform was arranged so that it could be jacked up as the tower construction proceeded.

The lifting routine was as follows: starting from a level position, the cross girder in the north and south columns was first lifted 6 inches, then the other end was lifted 1 ft, then the first end 1 ft, and so on until 16 lifts had been made, after which a final lift of 6 inches at the end first lifted made the platform level again. When the platforms had been lifted to a sufficient height, riveting cages were suspended from their undersides and drawn up with the platforms in subsequent lifts. Each cage consisted of a circular wire cylinder placed around a riveting machine. Inside the cages the men worked with perfect safety as regards falling or dropping tools etc. on workers below. The vertical columns were always built above the platforms to the maximum height that could be reached with the cranes, while the diagonal struts were built above or below the platforms as appropriate.

The platform on the Inchgarvie tower weighed 700 tons and required an additional central support. The first lift of the Inchgarvie platform, for various reasons, took nearly 18 days during January and February 1887—the last lift on 9 August 1887 was accomplished in 5 hours.

Work on the construction of the towers continued night and day as far as weather conditions permitted; numerous electric lamps were provided for the purpose (Fig. 3.14). It is interesting to note the attention paid to detail at the connections of the main members. At the main intersections at the top of the towers, a large number of longitudinal web plates (diaphragms) were introduced into the tubular and other members. Thus, the load in the members was gradually transferred from the outside circular shell plating into the longitudinal diaphragms and thence back into the other members intersecting at the point.

Erection of the main towers was completed in the summer of 1887 (Fig. 3.15). The final removal of the erection platforms, many hundred tons in weight, was a job which caused considerable anxiety, as men were working on nearly every portion of the structure below, and the fall of even a small bolt or nut could have been fatal. The year in which the central towers were erected showed the greatest number of fatal accidents (17); the annual average over the 7 years was nine.

The next task was the construction of the cantilever sections (Fig. 3.16). A crane was positioned near the skewback, and erected some 100 ft of tube. A rectangular cage was then constructed at the front end of the tube, which carried the riveting machine with sufficient room for the men to work in. On top of this structure a hydraulic crane was fixed, which lifted out the next plates. Rails were built on the top of the tube, and a carriage used to pull the material to a point where it could be reached by the crane (Fig. 3.17).

A link tie was erected to support the bottom tube, and this was followed by

the main plate tie (Fig. 3.18). As the construction progressed, the cranes at the top of the towers and those on the railway viaduct were used.

Work also proceeded on the top cantilever members connected to the tops of the towers. At the end of each member was a platform and a lifting appliance. The exposed position of the men can be fully appreciated, and their work through cold and windy weather was a feat of great endurance. The cantilevers continued to be constructed in balance using a workforce of some 3600 men (Figs 3.19–3.21).

All the rivets were heated in oil fired furnaces which gave excellent control, were easy to use and averted the danger of fire. The final sections of the suspended spans were fixed at their centres in November 1889 (Fig. 3.22).

One interesting aspect of the Forth Bridge construction was the use of steel wire ropes, a relatively recent innovation at the time the project commenced, which progressively superseded iron chains and hemp rope. Their reliability and much superior strength per unit weight proved most advantageous at all stages of the construction. For example, a steel wire rope of 4 inch circumference weighed 12 lbs per fathom, while a cable chain of the same strength weighed 54 lbs and a hemp rope 33 lbs. Similarly, a 2¼ inch

Fig. 3.21. View of construction: spring 1889

circumference wire rope weighed 3¾ lbs compared with 21 lbs for the chain and 11 lbs for the hemp rope.

Regarding visits to the construction, Mr Westhofen reports:

'As in most other matters, ladies were to the fore pluckily climbing into every nook and corner where anything interesting might be seen or learned, up the hoists and down the stairs and ladders and frequently leaving the members of the so-called stronger sex far behind. It is needless to say that, under these circumstances, the duties of those called upon to guard the fair visitors were of the most agreeable.

Rates of payment ranged from 4½ d an hour for labourers to 8 d an hour for platers. Some riveters made up to £3 per week, but the average wage was £2. These rates attracted travelling men who ranged the country looking for such work. There was an approximately equal split between English, Scottish and Irish workers. Foreign workers were also employed, who worked on the foundations and laid asphalt on the footpaths of the permanent way.

During the eight years of work, 57 men were killed. A Sick and Accident Club was formed which received contributions from both the men and the

Fig. 3.22. Suspended span construction: summer 1889

management. The number of workers employed varied throughout the contract from 2900 in winter to a maximum of 4600 in the summer of 1888. The weather had a major effect on the work; there were many gales, and at other times fog was a problem.

To test the completed structure in January 1890 two trains were taken on to the bridge, each with 50 loaded coal wagons, with three locomotives each weighing 73 tons at both ends of each train, making a gross weight of 1800 tons. The trains were run abreast but not allowed to cross to the other side. Measurements of the deflections showed that they were within the anticipated limits, about 7 inches at the ends of the cantilevers. During the test loading a severe gale was blowing, but this appeared to have little effect. The Board of Trade issued a certificate confirming its satisfaction with the tests, and a special passenger train crossed the bridge on 24 January 1890 carrying the chairmen of the various railway companies.

The bridge was formally opened by HRH The Prince of Wales accompanied by Prince George and the Dukes of Edinburgh and Fife, who crossed by train on 4 March 1890 and then declared the bridge open. At the ceremony the Prince announced that Queen Victoria had conferred knighthoods on William Arrol and Benjamin Baker for their work on the Tay and Forth Bridges. John Fowler had previously been knighted.

The Forth Bridge has continued to serve its purpose, and today carries far heavier trains than those for which it was designed. At the time of its completion it was the largest girder type bridge in the world, and held this distinction for more than 25 years, until the completion of the Quebec bridge in 1917.

Acknowledgements

The Author would like to express his grateful thanks to the following for permission to publish illustrations: The Principal Archivist, Strathclyde Regional Archives; British Rail Board Records Office; Moubray House Publishing, Edinburgh; and NEI Thompson Ltd.

CHAPTER 4

Maintaining the bridge

D. Grant, *Area Civil Engineer, ScotRail, Edinburgh*

The purpose of this Chapter is not to provide a lot of technical detail—instead, I hope to show that far from having a tired 100 year old structure to maintain, which might give countless problems, we have inherited from our distinguished predecessors a bridge which, given reasonable care and maintenance, will last for another 100 years.

The Forth Bridge (Fig. 4.1) carries around 200 trains every 24 hours; approximately 14½ million tons and 3 million passengers a year. The double track has reversible signalling on each line, and for track maintenance purposes we have Sunday daytime possession of one line available virtually every week if we wish to use it.

There are three speed restrictions on the bridge (Fig. 4.2):

50 mph for sprinters and high speed trains
40 mph for conventional diesel-hauled trains
30 mph for freight trains with axle loads of up to 22½ tons.

25 ton axle loads, the highest permitted on British Rail, are not allowed on the bridge, but occasional requests for trains with 25 ton axle load wagons, which have somehow ended up at Inverkeithing, come to the on-call engineer—usually in the early hours of the morning! We allow such a train over at 5 mph, with one or two well-chosen words of annoyance.

For the purpose of elucidation, aspects of the bridge can be separated as follows: masonry piers, approach spans, cantilevers, suspended spans, internal viaduct, track and staffing, accommodation etc.

Masonry piers

There are 15 piers in all, i.e. nine on the approach from South Queensferry, four on the approach from North Queensferry, and two main cantilever piers. In addition, there are four masonry arches at the extreme south end and three at the north end.

There are also the 4 piers to each of the three erections (Queensferry, Inchgarvie and Fife) founded on rock, or on boulder clay (for South Queensferry). Specialists are employed to inspect the underwater portions of the piers. The most recent inspection was in March 1989; another is due in the autumn of this year. The divers take video film of anything which looks even remotely suspect, and we can then examine the video together with their report. Due to the strong tides in the Firth, this inspection takes almost a week as there is only 1 hour's still water between tides. The timing of the inspection, of course, varies according to tidal patterns. Tides are normally about 18 ft, exceptionally 22 ft. In 1986, a hole about 4 ft deep just above very low tide level was discovered, which had been caused by the gradual corroding away of part of the outer ⅜ inch thick plate forming the top of the permanent caisson. As far can be seen, an unknown thickness (probably 9 inches) of brickwork was built against the iron sides of the caisson before it was filled with Arbroath stone and concrete. The action of the sea surging against the brick caused the hole to enlarge. It was prepared by infilling with concrete between tides. Sounding the plates from time to time will ensure quick action if any other holes develop.

Very little attention is required to the approach span or main piers above the water mark. The original specification stated that no external joint in the granite facing was to be more than ⅛ inch thick. Because the work was carried out in a very workmanlike manner, little pointing work has been necessary—when we stone cleaned the main cantilever pier towers by dry

Fig. 4.1. The Forth Bridge

Fig. 4.2. (above) Speed indicators

Fig. 4.3. (left) Stone-cleaned portal

Fig. 4.4. Sheeted bays of approach spans

grit blasting in 1987–88, funded by the Railway Heritage Trust, some minimal pointing work was required (Fig. 4.3). As far as we know there has been no noticeable degradation of the granite over 100 years.

When a plaque presented jointly by the American Society of Civil Engineers and the Institution of Civil Engineers was to be mounted on the pier facing the Hawes Inn in 1985, I engaged a reputable firm of monumental sculptors to prepare the stone. The foreman said he had to use seven or eight specially tipped masonry bits to drill the four holes for fixing bolts. More recently, 3 hours were taken to drill six holes for the new plaque commemorating the centenary.

The main towers, which are hollow in section, have given no known problems. There is a crack in the south masonry tower on the centre of the inshore face, extending upwards about six courses from the sand surrounding the base of the pier at low water, which we are planning to tab when weather conditions allow. (I tried to get a photo of this recently, but I doubt if the Maid of the Forth would have ventured out, far less my Rescue Boat!)

Approach spans

The steelwork is generally in good condition, although on the north approach viaduct the bottom bracing is showing some corrosion because of damp conditions under the timber walkway. We shall remove the timber walkway and, after any necessary steelwork repairs, replace it with galvanized steel walkway sections. At present we have a grit blasting and painting programme which has been running since early 1989, in which year we completed three bays on span 1, four on span 2, three on span 3, two on span 4, and three on span 5—span 6 is to be scaffolded in 1990. These are on the south side approach (Fig. 4.4).

Despite an expensive sheeting programme, to allow our own men to work in all weathers but chiefly for environmental reasons, we got specks into the summer ice-creams of South Queensferry. Given an east wind there were some problems of dust and so on blowing out from the top of the sheeted area. Various tests were done with the District Environmental Health people, who in the end gave us a clean bill of health. Our programme will continue— fortunately beyond reach of the public—but it will take about another 10 years to get all the way across the bridge before starting again!

We have 145 acres of paintwork, 120 of them, at a guess, external. The grit blasting and painting are done where we are trying to ensure that we don't have to come back to an area for at least 12 years. A five coat system is involved—after dry grit blasting and any necessary steelwork repairs, the whole surface is given a brushed-on primer coat within 4 hours of blasting, followed up by two coats of undercoat and two of Forth Bridge red paint (still supplied by Craig and Rose) (Fig. 4.5).

All four coats are sprayed on with airless spray equipment, which gives a very even coating. There is a colour code so that we can instantly recognise which coat has last been applied. Primer is yellow, first undercoat light green, second dark green, first top coat dark grey, and the final coat, of course, is Forth Bridge red. No red or white lead paints are now used.

Other parts of the bridge might only be chipped with compressed air chipping hammers before getting the same paint treatment. Parts where there are no signs of paint decay get only a top coat or coats. Because of drift it may

Fig. 4.5. Preparation of steelwork

Fig. 4.6. Wing stage

not be possible to spray paint unless we can protect the site by sheeting, so much of the paint is brushed on—the painters have strong arms and wrists! The final coats are to a comparatively new formula—toluenated vinyl alkyl. I'm no chemist, but the results are excellent and the new systems will, I am sure, give at least twice the life of previous paints.

Returning to the approach spans: the walkways are asphalted, and although they are in fairly good condition, there are some very uneven portions. We have experimental non-slip surfaces which were laid in the late 1970s, and these show potential for the future replacement of asphalt. However, with budgets being particularly tight at the moment, the existing walkways will have to last a bit longer. The cost of complete renewal would be in the region of over £2 million.

There are wing stages (Fig. 4.6) which have been in place since time immemorial, running on the teak wind-fence rail; at present these are our only means of getting over the side to reach the holding down saddle bolts which secure the longitudinal timbers. We are considering a new design.

Cantilevers

While some of the paintwork on the main tubes is looking quite scruffy, the sheer thickness of metal is a saviour! Our problem has been financial. To comply with Health and Safety at Work Act 1974, and to avoid an unsightly appearance, we have had to develop ways of overcoming such difficulties as painting the underside of the main tubes. Under the old system, two painters were lowered down on bosun's chairs—one on either side—and when down far enough they started swinging towards each other, finally meeting and attaching a chain between them ('Haul away Jimmy!'). Those on top then pulled them up to painting distance, and they started chipping and painting. Once that patch was finished, some chain was loosened off—up again—chip, paint and so on. Various planks, rope ladders and other dangerous looking practices were used up to 1974.

We have now fitted stools to the tops of the tubes (Fig. 4.7), and have temporary rails bolted to them along which a stout bogie arrangement can be winched. Supported from a cantilever system, we can then sling a cradle from which a complete section can be chipped and painted at a time in safety. The insides of the tubes were originally painted with white lead (Fig. 4.8). No one working on the bridge can recall when they were last painted—probably about 35 years ago, but the paintwork is in excellent condition. It is, I believe, a chloride rubber based paint. We test under the Entry to Confined Spaces code for oxygen level before entering tubes. The verticals and diagonal columns require a different technique with a suspended cradle fitted with adjustable rollers to take up the play. The top members are treated in much the same way as the bottom booms, again with cradles suspended from a trolley on stools. The struts, of which there are twelve to each cantilever, i.e.

Fig. 4.7. (left) Stool

Fig. 4.8. (right) Interior of tube

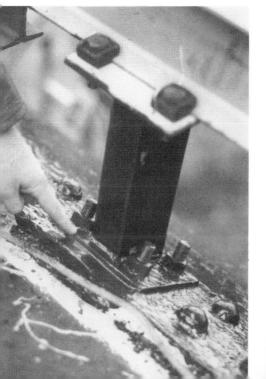

Fig. 4.9. *(above) Cradling*

Fig. 4.10. *(right) Cradling*

72 in all, we will get to in late 1990, mostly by hanging cradles (Figs 4.9 and 4.10), but perhaps by scaffolding on the lower parts.

The struts give the greatest problem because of the three-dimensional factors—inclination equivalent to 1 in 7½ in end elevation, at angles varying from about 32–62° to the vertical in elevation. The 'S'-bracing, i.e. the lattice girders connecting the verticals springing from the piers, over land on the Fife erection, is having a complete replacement of some 6 × 6 inch angle diagonal bracing at present, and is being given the five coat treatment. Inchgarvie and Queensferry 'S'-bracings will be tackled next. Scaffolding will be by boat initially; working from land will give us experience in the techniques needed over water.

The top bedplate to which the skewback is riveted was designed to allow it to have sliding movement relative to the bottom bedplate. Lubricating points were provided, but I am convinced that no movement has ever taken place! I believe that the last attempt to lubricate was about 3 years ago. I have to admit that I discovered only from material in Chapter 2 of this volume that the sliding arrangement was provided solely for the construction period.

There are 2 radar reflecting discs on the Inchgarvie tower which are the responsibility of the Forth Ports Authority. When in 1989 the authority complained of a poor picture it was discovered that one of the discs had blown away!

Fig. 4.11. Pin connecting suspended span to cantilever

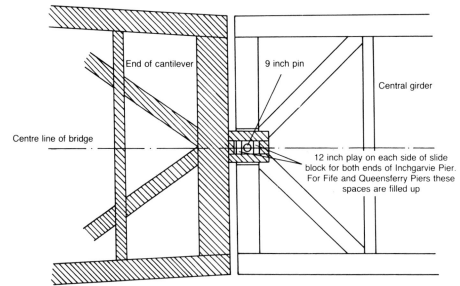

Fig. 4.12. (right) Position of top pin

Fig. 4.13. (below) Lifting maintenance stages up to bridge

Connections between cantilevers and suspended spans

These connections are basically pinned joints, and the pins are quite remarkable! (Fig. 4.11). When it was decided some years ago to investigate the condition of one of them, various attempts were made to coax out the bottom pin on the Inchgarvie cantilever to the south suspended span. I have to admit that there was no way the pin could be persuaded to move, in spite of many attempts, and frankly we are no wiser today as to the condition of the joints. Perhaps we should try again on some future occasion—any sensible ideas would be welcome! However, we are reassured by the massive size of the pins and the arrangement into which they fit. There is no apparent movement of the pins in the holes (Fig. 4.12).

Suspended spans

The suspended spans are in good condition, and do not cause much difficulty in painting. Up above and on the side girders, the painters scramble with safety harness. Travelling maintenance stages were erected to cover the bottom members in the 1970s, and give no problems. These are hand-cranked (Fig. 4.13) to the correct position and have hand-pumped hydraulic brakes. If

Fig. 4.14. (below left) Old walkways

Fig. 4.15. (below right) New walkways

a taller than usual ship is due, we are notified from Rosyth and have to shift the stage from the centre.

Navigation lights are fitted—red at either end of each suspended span and white in the centre. These used to be examined by the watchmen, but now have a multi-bulb system which sounds an alarm in the Edinburgh Signalling Centre when the second last bulb comes on. The lighthouse on Bouch's pier is also maintained by us, and requires little attention. There can be problems, though, in getting to the lighthouse in heavy weather to repair or change the light bulbs.

Internal viaduct

The internal viaduct was strengthened between 1913 and 1921; a paper on this operation was presented to the Institution of Civil Engineers in 1922. In general, the viaduct is in good condition—minor steelwork repairs are part of normal maintenance requirements. Two areas, however, tend to demand on-going maintenance/renewal.

(a) *The trough girders* composed of plates and angles, which carry the rail supported on oak logs, have given some cause for concern over the years. The bottom plates have shown signs of fatigue cracking under the fairly heavy axle loads (22½ tons) which the bridge now carries. For over 20 years repairs have been conducted by welding on additional steel bottom plates. These seem to have been very effective, as no cracking has occurred in the new plates. The work is on-going, carried out by contract let on an annual basis.

(b) *The walkways* (Figs 4.14 and 4.15) along the foot of the internal viaduct (one on each side) are supported by the bottom cross members and are basically 15 x 2 inch timber, bolted on. A taut wire handhold is provided on each side. Rot in the timber and retention of water under the planks at holding down points has in some cases caused severe corrosion of the steelwork—a programme is now in place for gradual replacement of the wooden walkways with steel, and as this work is undertaken so are any repairs required on the steelwork. We use Eurogrid galvanized steel sections. We are implementing a similar policy on the top booms where, in fact, the Inchgarvie cantilever is complete—we are working on Queensferry South cantilever at present. There are many ladders on the bridge, some of which we are gradually replacing with modern standard safety ladders in the most essential positions. The use of power cradles has in some cases reduced the need for ladders—those to one and two top ties are being abandoned and will eventually be recovered for scrap.

Track

The actual rail on which the trains run is carried on longitudinal waybeams rather than traditional ballasted track. These in turn are inside trough girders

Fig. 4.16. Sorting logs

which form an integral part of the internal viaduct. The 'logs', as we call the waybeams, are 28 ft long and are mostly oak, although there are some jarrah logs. They need to be tailored to fit each site by adzing etc.—there are 1184 altogether. Each log has traditionally been supported on oak packers, but in the last 6 years composition rubber/cork bounded packers have been used (Fig. 4.16). In turn, the logs (nominally 14 × 9 inches) support the rails which are held at the correct level and inclination (1 in 20) by further packing pieces, again mainly of oak, rubber/cork bonded pads having been introduced since 1984. A 25 year life span means that 50 per year, i.e. two per Sunday for half the year, need to be renewed, at a material cost of almost £500 each. They are dated as they go in—the oldest logs have been in for 26–27 years. The rails are 126 lb/yard and 4¼ inches in depth, the foot width being 8½ inches, and are traditional 'Forth Bridge' rails drilled every 2 ft on either side of the foot and staggered by 3 inches to allow them to be coach screwed down to the logs. They are ultrasonically tested every 6 months.

Expansion switches, of which there are four long and seven short on each road, are manufactured out of 146 lb/yard section. We are now running short of this heavy section rail, and hope to find an alternative design in the near future. Even the 126 lb rails are running slightly low in stock; an alternative will be required in the next 5 years. Compatibility with existing rails is an important requirement.

Rail level is about 1½ inches below the top of walkway level, and there have been some problems in the past with locomotive snowploughs occasionally striking the walkway top. This could be further aggravated by the new design of 158 Sprinter snowploughs, and is the subject of discussion with our mechanical engineering and business colleagues. If we raise rail level, there is likely to be a clearance problem for 8 ft 6 inches containers on conventional wagons, and for any future plans, however distant, for electrification of the line over the bridge. If we retain or renew the rails at the present level, can the snowplough difficulty be overcome? As mentioned above, complete renewal of the walkways would cost in the region of £2 million. A cheaper solution may be the provision of hard rubber inserts on the snowplough extremities.

The average age of rail on the bridge is probably about 30 years, and rail flaws in the older rails become more of a problem year after year. Heavy axle loads contribute to this, fatigue being the most likely cause of flaws. About 16 rail faults have been dealt with this year, mostly squats (hydrogen inclusions forming cracks on the running table of the rail).

The rails are not fishplated together in the normal way—the joints are supported for line and level by a rail baseplate which is itself screwed to the log. Any deterioration of the log can create more deflection of the rail ends

Fig. 4.17. Forth Bridge Supervisor

than the design permits, causing rail end fatigue. There are also special joints where the rail at each end of the bridge connects to standard British Rail rail.

Cost

The total annual cost of maintaining the bridge is about £1 million, broken down roughly as follows:

Labour	£450 000
Materials	
Paint	£15 000
Other	£50 000
Contracts	
Cradling	£350 000
Trough girder strengthening	£75 000
Other steelwork repairs	£25 000

Forth Bridge staff

How do we organize work on the bridge? I have a Forth Bridge Manager, a Bridge Supervisor (Fig. 4.17) and a Bridge Foreman who all work from the Forth Bridge office opened in August 1984. They have an office shopman who does the clerical work and mans the radio, which links directly with the bridge staff and the rescue boat. The latter, a Searider inshore rescue with twin 25 hp Evinrude outboards is based at our own slipway at North Queensferry and is manned constantly when staff are working. It can cross the river in less than a minute. A new boat, recently delivered, is self-righting in the event of a capsize. Unfortunately it won't fit through the boathouse doorway, being about 2 inches too tall when on the cradle. Just another little problem to overcome!

The remainder of the Forth Bridge staff comprises

24 painters (should be 28)

7 riggers

5 permanent way men

1 joiner

2 boatmen.

The painters are usually organized in gangs of 4.

The Forth estuary is notorious for wind: during a very pleasant breezy day at Dalmeny Station, a 60 mph wind might be blowing at the top of the bridge. Hand held anemometers are used to gauge wind strength, and if winds are over 40 mph no work is done from cradles. In former times only 90–100 days in the year could be worked on stagings or cradles. Now, with protective sheeting, we can work in several locations in all but the worst gales. Admittedly we've lost quite a few so far in 1990!

There is portacabin accommodation for the men at Dalmeny, with showers available after dirty work. Health and Safety at Work regulations require this,

Fig. 4.18. (right) Bothies on transom

Fig. 4.19. (below) Interior of bothy

and we test all Forth Bridge staff twice a year for blood lead levels. Only one is category B, not a danger level but requiring vigilance. Hygiene is the most important aspect of managing this potential problem.

There are bothies on the bridge at each erection, the Inchgarvie bothy having been modernized fairly recently, and giving a good standard of accommodation for men at break times (Figs 4.18 and 4.19). Flush toilets are provided, but those of the sailing fraternity should beware! To get materials out on to the bridge we have a diesel–hydraulic tug unit that can haul a short train of wagons. We are in fact awaiting delivery of a new, more powerful system with a Hyab crane unit which will make life a lot easier—at present most materials have to be manhandled.

One thing I have wanted for several years is electrical power on the bridge. We use portable compressors for air tools, and diesel generators for bothies, cradle power lifts and some of the electric 110 V hand tools are used on the Permanent Way. The transportation of diesel in barrels is time-consuming (and unpopular).

I made a case for full power supply on the bridge about 4 years ago. The idea would be to have take-off points at regular distances throughout the bridge, where electrically driven compressors would supply the air tools, and transformers would provide the 110 V supply for lighting and portable power

Fig. 4.20. An unusual view—the bridge that goes nowhere!

tools. The large capital cost meant that the pay-back would have been over a long period, and in any case the capital was not then available, so my scheme foundered. There may, however, be a glimmer of light (pardon the pun) associated with the floodlighting of the bridge during this Centenary year.

I hope I have conveyed some idea of maintenance problems, or, even better, the absence of problems on the bridge (Fig. 4.20). After all, as my Bridge Manager has been quoted as saying recently, 'It's only a bridge, not a bloody circus!' But quite a bridge nevertheless, and our pride and joy.

CHAPTER 5

The men behind the bridge

R. M. Birse, *Department of Civil Engineering and Building Science, Edinburgh University*

Everyone with any interest in engineering will have their own mental picture of 'the men behind the bridge'; some may think only of the big names, Fowler, Baker and Arrol; others may remember also the shadowy Sir Thomas Tancred, his partner Travers Falkiner, Evelyn Carey the photographer and Wilhelm Westhofen the writer of the account that appeared in *Engineering*.

The commemorative portrait group (Fig. 5.1) which appeared at the time of the bridge's completion includes all the Directors of the Forth Bridge Railway Company and all senior staff employed by Fowler and Baker, and Tancred and Arrol—a total of 49 men. And surely no-one could forget the thousands of men (and boys) who laboured on the building of the bridge (Fig. 5.2), though very few of their names are known today. However, an army several thousand strong notwithstanding, some of the most important men behind the bridge have still not been mentioned—the men who had developed the science and practice of civil engineering to a level where, towards the end of the nineteenth century, the construction of such an outstanding bridge became possible for the first time.

Taking a broad view of the Forth Bridge in its conception and realization, therefore, it seemed to me that the men behind the bridge could be separated into six categories, each one distinguished by its own raison d'être, as follows.

Men of vision, driven by the urge to foresee the future
Men of substance, driven by the urge to acquire wealth and status
Men of learning, driven by the urge to acquire knowledge
Men of ingenuity, driven by the urge to make things work
Men of skill, driven by the urge to make things better
Men of muscle, driven by the urge to eat and drink!

The men of vision
The men who saw in the early years of the nineteenth century that the Firth of Forth could be crossed by a tunnel or a bridge instead of the hazardous ferry

passage were just a few decades ahead of their time. In fact Richard Trevithick's abortive attempt to drive a tunnel beneath the Thames was already under way in 1805 when John Grieve of Edinburgh proposed the idea of a tunnel under the Forth, with William Vazie and James Taylor as his associates in the venture.

James Anderson, an Edinburgh civil engineer and surveyor, published in 1818 his *Report on bridge of chains to be thrown over the Firth of Forth at Queensferry*, a project which was much farther ahead of its time than the tunnel. Details of both of these schemes, which must have given rise to much discussion and speculation at the time, can be found in Chapter 1.

From the point of view of the Forth Bridge itself, the men of vision, who saw that it could, should, and indeed must be built, were the successive Chairmen of the North British Railway, Richard Hodgson and John Stirling of Kippendavie, and the sometime engineer of the Edinburgh, Perth and Dundee Railway, Thomas Bouch. Their part in the eventual achievement of the crossing of the Forth is described below.

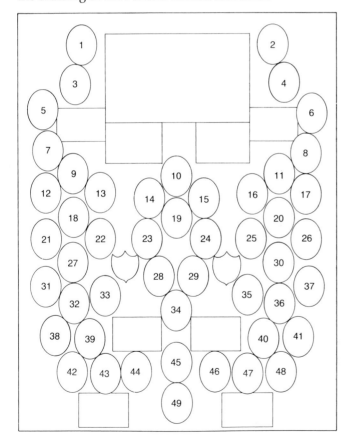

1. Arthur J. Knowles
2. James Blackburn
3. Sir William Arrol
4. Sir Benjamin Baker
5. Joseph Phillips
6. Frederick E. Cooper
7. Andrew S. Biggart
8. William N. Bakewell
9. A. J. Symonds
10. Marquis of Tweeddale
11. Spencer Brunton
12. Reginald E. Middleton
13. P. Walter Meik
14. Sir M. W. Ridley
15. William U. Heygate
16. Samuel Balbirnie
17. Thomas Scott
18. Louis Neville
19. Lord Colville
20. Walter S. Bourke
21. Duncan Campbell
22. Rudolph Lilliquist
23. Sir M. W. Thompson
24. Earl of Elgin
25. Wilhelm Westhofen
26. George Aitken
27. Alex Chalmers
28. James Hall Renton
29. Lord Hindlip
30. Sir Maurice Fitzmaurice
31. T. Main
32. Allan D. Stewart
33. Sir Ernest W. Moir
34. John Dent Dent
35. E. Malcolm Wood
36. Axel Schluter
37. Adam Hunter
38. William Gray
39. Alfred E. Mavor
40. Evelyn Carey
41. J. B. Webster
42. James E. Tuit
43. John Walker
44. William White Millar
45. G. B. Wieland
46. John Noble
47. Sir Henry Oakley
48. David Harris
49. Sir John Fowler
Shields: Sir T. Tancred,
T. H. Falkiner, J. Law, J. Martin
Omitted: L. Coiseau,
K. Watanabe

Fig. 5.1 (left and facing) Commemorative portrait group

Fig. 5.2. Riveting . . . at a dizzy height, but note boy at lower right . . .

The men of substance

If it took men of vision to dream up plans for cavernous tunnels and spidery suspension bridges, it was in the end only through the efforts of the men of substance that a bridge across the Forth was successfully completed. It certainly required a great deal of the solid Victorian virtues of ambition and determination to create a bridge that in one stride took structural engineering firmly into the twentieth century.

The advent of the railways in the middle of the nineteenth century transformed the transport scene in Britain and throughout the Western World. Roads and road bridges had never been profitable even when tolls were charged; indeed road users to this day resent direct charges on what most people regard as their natural right of free movement. The canals of the eighteenth century heralded the first transport revolution, and many of them were moderately successful as commercial enterprises; in some other countries canals still form a valuable part of the transport infrastructure.

The railways introduced a completely new dimension to the movement of both goods and people, the dimension of speed, for which industrialists especially were willing to pay a substantial premium. The railway companies promised a good return on capital, and in the second half of the nineteenth century most of them had no difficulty in attracting investors to finance the construction of new lines or the acquisition of competing ones. It was in this climate of expansion and competition that the North British Railway, with its networks of lines in south-east Scotland and Fife and with running powers over the Caledonian line north to Aberdeen, knew that in order to survive, let alone prosper, it had to build railway bridges over the Tay and Forth estuaries.

The North British Railway had been founded in 1844 at the instigation of John Learmonth, then Chairman of the very successful Edinburgh and Glasgow Railway, who could see the advantages that would accrue from a connection between the Scottish railways and the rapidly growing lines south of the border. The initial aim of the North British was to build a line from Edinburgh to Berwick-on-Tweed, on which no fewer than five trains a day were running by the summer of 1846, two of them connecting with the coaches that still ran from Berwick to Newcastle. Excursions were run from both Edinburgh and Glasgow to 'England', and the wondering travellers were made doubly certain that they had entered a foreign country by the customs officers at Berwick who insisted on searching their baggage and confiscating any 'colonial liquors' such as Scotch whisky!

After an auspicious start, the North British went through a period of considerable difficulty: the main line to Berwick had been constructed too quickly with shoddy materials and workmanship, and landslips and floods put it out of action on several occasions. Too many branch lines were built on which the traffic never justified the expenditure, and to cap it all the great

Fig. 5.3. (above) James Clerk Maxwell (1831–79)

Fig. 5.4. (above right) W. J. McQuorn Rankine (1820–72).

predator George Hudson, the 'Railway King', set out to add the North British to his 'empire'. To his credit, Learmonth succeeded where many other railway chairmen had failed, and Hudson abandoned the fight.

At about the same time as the east and west coast routes from London to Edinburgh and Glasgow were completed in 1850, chairmanship of the North British passed to Richard Hodgson of Carham Hall, Coldstream—just on the English side of the River Tweed. With two other Englishmen, Thomas Rowbotham and William Hurst, as general manager and locomotive superintendent, Hodgson set out to restore the fortunes of the ailing North British. It has to be said that he did so by every means in his power, including some double dealing with the Caledonian Railway and some very dubious accounting practices. *The Times* said: 'As a railway director he is one of the daring, dashing ambitious class, a man who appears to look on shareholders as mere tools and puppets of an imperial will', and the *Spectator* called him 'Resolute, remorseless and one-idea'd, a man utterly unscrupulous when needful, yet always strictly economical of unscrupulousness.'

By the time he was finally voted out of office in 1866, 'King Richard'

Hodgson had built the 'Waverley' line through the Scottish borders from Edinburgh to Carlisle, had acquired a number of other border lines, and had taken over the Edinburgh, Perth and Dundee Railway in 1862 and the Edinburgh and Glasgow Railway in 1865. Under his forceful leadership the North British Railway had grown from a 58 mile main line with a few short branches to a network of 781 miles of track stretching from Berwick and Carlisle to Edinburgh, Glasgow, Perth, Dundee and Aberdeen.

A glance at a map of the east coast of Scotland is enough to show the importance of the Tay and Forth estuaries. Long before its takeover by the North British, the Edinburgh, Perth and Dundee Railway had inaugurated the world's first train ferries in 1849, from Granton to Burntisland and from Tayport to Broughty Ferry. The idea for these specially built paddle-steamers, as well as the design of the movable slipways for loading and unloading the waggons, came from the fertile mind of the company's manager and engineer at the time, Thomas Bouch.

The train ferries were certainly ingenious, but were used only for goods waggons, and both Thomas Bouch (who in 1852 had resigned to practise as a consulting civil engineer) and the new Chairman of the North British, John Stirling of Kippendavie, were determined to bridge the Tay and the Forth as soon as possible. In the end the Tay had to be bridged not once but twice; the even greater expense entailed in bridging the Forth was clearly beyond the resources of the North British alone.

Kippendavie (as he was generally known) therefore approached the three English railway companies most likely to benefit from the building of the Forth Bridge—the North-Eastern, the Great Northern and the Midland—and together they formed the Forth Bridge Railway Company for the specific purpose of building and operating the Forth Bridge. The directors of the new company comprised two men from each of the constituent companies together with a further two elected by the shareholders, and Westhofen[1] listed them at the time of the bridge's completion as:

Mr (later Sir) Matthew William Thompson (Chairman) and Mr William Unwin Heygate (Midland Railway Company)
Lord Colville of Culross and Lord Hindlip (Great Northern Railway Company)
Mr John Dent Dent (Deputy Chairman) and Sir Matthew White Ridley, Bart (North-Eastern Railway Company)
The Marquis of Tweeddale and the Earl of Elgin and Kincardine (North British Railway Company)
Mr Spencer Brunton and Mr James Hall Renton representing the shareholders.

These were the men of substance, the men without whose backing the Forth Bridge would not have been built at that time.

The men of learning

This is perhaps the right place to emphasise that a complex structure such as the Forth Bridge should not be considered as the creation of two or three men, not even of all those men who were engaged on its actual design and construction. The science and practice of bridge building had been developing for centuries before the level of knowledge and experience that made the Forth Bridge possible was attained. The achievement of Fowler, Baker, Arrol and their colleagues is not diminished in acknowledging their debt to the generations of scientists, engineers and craftsmen who preceded them.

Engineering is an applied science as well as an applied art, and most engineers are too busy applying what little science they can remember from their student days to have time to pursue any fundamental research—they quite rightly leave that to the scientists, on whom they rely for the theoretical principles they try to put into practice.

So who were the men of learning behind the analysis and design of the Forth Bridge? There were, of course, hundreds if not thousands, from Euclid and Archimedes, through Leonardo and Newton, to Euler and Coulomb and Navier and Saint-Venant, to name but a few. But if we must take one man as an archetypal scientist, a man driven by the urge to find out, who better to choose than James Clerk Maxwell (Fig. 5.3)?[2] Besides, he happens to be one of *us*, born in Edinburgh in 1831. Clerk Maxwell died in 1879 at the age of only 48—had he lived, he would have been just 59 when the Forth Bridge was opened in 1890. As a child, he showed insatiable curiosity and an exceptional memory, yet was regarded at school (the Edinburgh Academy) as shy and rather dull—later in life, recalling his unhappy schooldays, he used to say with a thin, sad smile: 'They never understood me; but I understood them'. He blossomed intellectually at about the age of 13, and entered the University of Edinburgh in 1847, proceeding to Trinity College, Cambridge in 1850.

In his short intensely productive life Clerk Maxwell wrote four books and about a hundred scientific papers. His discovery and mathematical exposition of the laws of electrodynamics was described by P. G. Tait in the *Encyclopedia Britannica* as 'One of the most splendid monuments ever raised by the genius of a single individual.' Einstein himself said 'To few men in the world has such an experience been vouchsafed.'

However, the laws of electrodynamics didn't help much (directly) to get the Forth Bridge built. Clerk Maxwell also made significant contributions to optics, photo-elasticity, colorimetry, astronomy, the kinetic theory of gases, molecular physics, *elasticity of materials*, and *graphical analysis of structural frameworks*—so he is indeed one of the many scientists behind the engineers behind the bridge.

Clerk Maxwell's 1864 paper 'On the calculation of the equilibrium and stiffness of frames' appeared in the *London, Edinburgh and Dublin Philosophical*

Magazine, which goes a long way to explain its lack of impact on the average structural engineer! Charlton notes that it 'is remarkable for the physical insight displayed, its brevity (without diagrams), breadth and originality'.[3]

It should perhaps be mentioned here that scientists and engineers tend to be different *kinds* of people, approaching the same problem in quite different ways, and not always or easily understanding one another's point of view. Most scientists prefer to express their problems and solutions in mathematical terms, while engineers are generally happier if they can 'see' a problem and its solution in graphical form.

What engineers need, very often, is an 'interpreter' who can translate the scientists' theories into down-to-earth engineering terms: such a one, in the middle of the nineteenth century, was another Edinburgh man, William John Macquorn Rankine (Fig. 5.4).[4] The son of an engineer, Rankine was born in 1820 and like Clerk Maxwell died relatively young, in 1872, aged only 52. He attended Ayr Academy and Glasgow High School, each for only one year due to illness. The rest of his education was imparted by his father and the occasional tutor at home. Nevertheless he matriculated at Edinburgh

Fig. 5.5. (below left) Sir John Fowler and his eldest grandson

Fig. 5.6. (below) Sir Benjamin Baker: with droopy would-be cantilever moustache!

University, where he was a gold medallist at the age of 16 for an essay on 'The undulatory theory of light'. After some years in practice as a civil engineer he was appointed in 1855 to the Regius Chair of Civil Engineering and Mechanics at the University of Glasgow, succeeding Lewis Gordon who in 1840 had been the first man appointed to an engineering chair in Britain.[5]

Rankine produced a steady stream of papers on thermodynamics, hydrodynamics and other theoretical subjects, but more importantly he wrote a series of manuals for practising engineers on *'Applied mechanics'* (1858), *'The steam engine and other prime movers'* (1859), *'Civil engineering'* (1862), *'Useful rules and tables'* (1866), *'Machinery and Millwork'* (1869), and the *'Cyclopedia of machine and hand tools'* (1869); he also edited *'Shipbuilding, theoretical and practical'* (1866).

These works provided engineers with the first comprehensive presentation of the fundamental theories of engineering science and their applications, and their popularity was such that they went into many editions over many years—the 27th edition of *'Civil engineering'* for example, appeared in about 1927 with additions and corrections by W. J. Millar, CE, the Secretary of the Institution of Engineers and Shipbuilders in Scotland. We can be sure that copies of Professor Rankine's Manuals were at the elbow of most of the engineers engaged in the design and construction of the Forth Bridge.

Men of ingenuity

The engineers

After the inevitable departure of Sir Thomas Bouch from the scene following the Tay Bridge disaster of December 1879, one of the first acts of the Forth Bridge Railway Company was to ask its consulting engineers to reconsider the feasibility of a Forth Railway Bridge, and if appropriate to recommend the type of bridge most suitable for the crossing. The men charged with this daunting task were William Henry Barlow of the Midland, Thomas Elliot Harrison of the North-Eastern, and John Fowler of the Great Northern.

William Barlow and his father Peter, himself a scientist and engineer of some repute, are mentioned in Chapter 1. Peter's eldest son Peter William Barlow, FRS (1809–1885), was a civil engineer who in 1855–8 studied the construction of long-span bridges in great detail, including a visit to Niagara, where Roebling had built the 250 m span road and rail suspension bridge that was in use until 1897.

Having served an apprenticeship at Woolwich dockyard, William was sent by Maudslay and Field to Constantinople in 1832, and on his return to England 6 years later became resident engineer on several railway contracts in the Midlands. With Sir John Hawkshaw he completed Brunel's Clifton suspension bridge in 1860, and he designed for the Midland Railway the 73 m span roof of St Pancras Station, the largest in Britain, completed in 1868. William Barlow was President of the Institution of Civil Engineers in 1879–80.

Fig. 5.7. Sir John Fowler, Lady Fowler (?) and Sir William Arrol

Thomas Harrison (1808–88) worked with Robert Stephenson in 1830–31 on the London and Birmingham Railway, and again in 1845–49 on the Newcastle to Berwick line. When the North-Eastern Railway was formed in 1854 he was appointed chief engineer, and built for it the Tyne Dock at South Shields and the swing bridges at Goole and Naburn near York. One of his greatest achievements was the splendid curving roof of the station at York, completed in 1877. Harrison was President of the Institution of Civil Engineers in 1873–74.

There is undoubtedly more biographical material on John Fowler (1817–98) (Fig. 5.5) than on any other man connected with the Forth Bridge, including a full-length biography by Mackay[6] and extended accounts in Refs 1, 7 and 8 and elsewhere. So much is readily available, in fact, that this is not the place to attempt more than a brief impression of Fowler's life while the bridge was under consideration and construction.

He had been a consulting engineer since the age of 26, rising rapidly on the tidal wave of the railway boom to the very top of his profession. His reputation was consolidated in the minds of his fellow engineers and the general public by his work on the construction of the Metropolitan Railway (which eventually became the Circle Line of the London Underground) in 1853–1865. Fowler was elected President of the Institution of Civil Engineers

Fig. 5.8. (above) Allan Duncan Stewart (1831–94)

Fig. 5.9. (above right) Sir William Arrol, aged about 36 (in 1875)

in January 1866.

It is worth remembering that Benjamin Baker (1840–1907) (Fig. 5.6) joined Fowler's staff in 1861 and became his partner in 1875 when Baker was 35 and Fowler already 58. The former had made a special study of long-span bridges early in his career, publishing a series of papers on the subject in *Engineering*;[9] there can be little doubt that the application of the cantilever principle to the Forth Bridge was primarily his idea. After due consideration this design was recommended by the consulting engineers and accepted by the North British Railway.

One of the many other theoretical and experimental investigations carried out by Baker had particular significance in the construction of the Forth Bridge: he proved that the then common practice of punching holes for the rivets in iron plates could severely damage them, and it was specified as a result that all the rivet holes in the Forth Bridge steelwork be drilled.

Many years before, in 1857, Fowler had bought an estate in the Highlands of Scotland, and in 1865–67 he purchased two adjacent estates in Ross-shire covering a total of some 40 000 acres. In his biography it is said he claimed 'that he had done his best to be a Scotsman'.[6] For 40 years of his life he never missed spending the autumns in Scotland, stalking his stags and fishing for salmon like any other Highland laird.

The following picture of Fowler[6] is provided by his junior partner Baker:

'I first met Sir John Fowler 40 years ago . . . (and) the impression I then formed of him is as clear today as ever, and has never varied. I felt myself in the presence of a born commander of men, who formed his opinion with instinctive quickness, held on to it firmly, never questioning its soundness himself, nor failing sooner or later to satisfy most of his hearers by ingenuity of argument and charm of manner, that if they held a contrary opinion originally it was a fortunate thing for them that they had come to see him before it was too late.'

It was undoubtedly Benjamin Baker who acted as partner-in-charge of the Forth Bridge contracts—in Ref. 7 it is stated that 'Throughout the long and arduous construction period, from 1883 to 1890, Baker practically lived on the site, where he took every available opportunity of carrying out valuable and interesting experiments on the mechanical properties of structural steel.'

Fig. 5.10. Joseph Phillips, Foreman (?), Mrs Arrol (?) and William Arrol: 2 March 1888

Fig. 5.11. Pumping out Queensferry caisson: note diver's helmet, air pumps and air lines, and diver(s) among men in background (September 1885)

Fowler of course was 66 years old when the work started in 1883 (Fig. 5.7), and for some years had been troubled by attacks of bronchitis, but he made every effort to pay fortnightly visits to the bridge, sometimes staying for several days at a time. On other occasions he escaped from the British winter to visit one of his sons who lived near Barcelona.

All the biographical sources tell us that Benjamin Baker was unmarried—when delivering this lecture I remarked that perhaps it was because he had no family (unlike Fowler and Arrol) that no biography of him had been written. After the lecture, however, a young American girl was introduced to me as 'Sir Benjamin Baker's great great grand-daughter', Amanda Movius by name. Apparently, although it is true that Baker never married, he did as a young man have a love affair with a Welsh girl as a result of which a daughter was born, though not before her outraged parents had taken her with them to the USA. For 8 years Baker did not even know where she was living, but eventually made contact with her again.

It is a well-known fact that, by late Victorian times at any rate, most Generals didn't actually *fight*, and by the same token most partners in civil engineering firms didn't actually *design* in any detail the projects for which they were nominally responsible. There is a passing reference on page 64 of Ref. 1 to a Mr Allen Stewart, and on page 69 it is stated that 'Mr Alan Stewart was chief of the staff in Westminster, where all the detailed drawings and calculations were made.' This sentence, however, only lifts a corner of the veil that hides the details of a very interesting career—the rest emerges when we read his obituary.[10]

Allan Duncan Stewart (Fig. 5.8) was surely a Scot, although his birthplace was not known to his obituarist. Born in 1831, he graduated 9th Wrangler in the Mathematical Tripos at Cambridge in 1853. From 1855 to 1858 he was articled to Benjamin Hall Blyth, a well-known Edinburgh consulting engineer, then for 2 years acted as resident engineer on the construction of the Banffshire Railway. In 1861 Stewart began to practise in Edinburgh as a consulting civil engineer, sometimes on his own account and sometimes for other engineers, working on railways, bridges (including that over the Tay at Grandtully), water supply and drainage.

Stewart was extensively employed in assisting Sir Thomas Bouch in the design and execution of several iron and steel bridges, where his high mathematical attainments and practical experience proved extremely useful. For Bouch he prepared the working drawings for the superstructure of the Redheugh (Newcastle upon Tyne) and Tay Bridges, for the roofs of Waverley (Edinburgh) and Dundee Stations, and for the steel piers, chains and girders of the proposed suspension bridge across the Firth of Forth. In 1880 he gave important evidence before the Royal Commission on the Tay Bridge disaster.

From 1881 to 1890 Stewart acted as Chief Assistant Engineer for Fowler and Baker on the design and construction of the Forth Bridge. He later practised in Westminster, and was again associated with Baker on the design of the Wembley Tower, but while engaged on this work he was struck down by illness and died in October 1894 at the age of 63. 'He was of a retiring disposition, and rarely attended the meetings of the Institution; but those of his professional brethren who knew him best most regret his loss.'

So ended his obituary, the story of a remarkable career. Allan Stewart must have had an unassailable reputation as a structural engineer to have emerged unscathed from his close association with Bouch and the first Tay Bridge, and it is surely the irony of ironies that he should almost immediately afterwards be employed by Fowler and Baker as their right-hand man on the design and construction of the Forth Bridge. One wonders what the public and the press might have thought and said if this had been widely known at the time.

In total, many dozens of engineers must have been engaged on the design of the Forth Bridge and on supervision of its construction—only a few others can be mentioned here. The Resident Engineers, first Patrick W. Meik (1883 to 1886), and second Frederick E. Cooper (1886 to 1890), were assisted by Evelyn Carey, who was also the official photographer to whom our grateful thanks are due for the superb series of progress photographs now preserved in the Imperial College of Science and Technology in London, and by Messrs Lilliquist, Tuit and Watanabe.

Kaichi Watanabe was the Japanese apprentice of Fowler and Baker who has passed into engineering history as the 'little man' who sits precariously between the large human cantilevers in Baker's famous illustration of the cantilever principle. Watanabe subsequently returned to Japan, where he became president of several railway companies.

Last of the engineers, but by no means least, we must pay special tribute to Reginald Middleton, the man who carried out the exacting task of triangulation before the start of work on site. Using a base line at South Queensferry 4000 ft in length, three points on the centre line of the bridge were set out, and their distances apart determined with the collaboration of the Ordnance Survey. Some 20 primary setting-out points were then carefully fixed for use in the construction of the bridge. Middleton had been articled to Robert Stephenson and Co. in Newcastle upon Tyne, and as well as being a Member

Fig. 5.12. South approach viaduct before raising

of the Institutions of Civil and Mechanical Engineers was a Fellow of the Surveyors' Institution.

Although not on Fowler and Baker's staff, it is appropriate to include here the two Board of Trade Inspectors who made quarterly inspections and submitted their reports on the construction of the Forth Bridge. Major-General Charles Scrope Hutchinson, RE was another of the small group of men who escaped censure after the collapse of the first Tay Bridge, largely because his final report allowing the bridge to be opened to traffic contained the vital sentence: 'I should wish if possible to have an opportunity of observing the effects of a high wind when a train of carriages is running over the bridge.'

Fig. 5.13. Raising viaduct girders, north approach: note nonchalant pose at convenient gap in line of washing! (September 1885)

Fig. 5.14. Skewback in fabrication yard

He never did have that opportunity; who knows what difference it might have made if he had? Anyway, both he and his colleague Major F. A. Marindin, along with the rest of the engineering profession, doubtless took many lessons from the Tay Bridge to heart, and in their first quarterly report on the Forth Bridge in June 1883 they wrote: 'Preparations indicate that it is the intention of the engineers and contractors to carry out the works in a manner suitable to the magnitude of the undertaking.' On that point they were quite correct.

The steelmakers

The Forth Bridge is often said to have been the first major bridge made entirely of steel, but that is true only in Europe—in fact the first major steel bridge was completed in 1874 by Captain James Buchanan Eads over the Mississippi River at St Louis, with three spans of 502 + 520 + 502 feet. The first man to produce steel in a Bessemer-type converter was also an American,

William Kelly, but after taking out a patent in 1857 he went bankrupt and Bessemer, who had been working independently along the same lines, made a fortune from his tilting converter which he patented in 1860.

Initially, however, the Bessemer process encountered serious teething troubles and there was much doubt about the quality of the steel produced, even after R. F. Mushet discovered the benefits of adding spiegeleisen to the molten steel. So when the alternative open-hearth method was introduced at about the same time it was adopted by many steel makers in preference to the Bessemer converter.[11]

Briefly, the men involved in the successful development of the Siemens–Martin open-hearth process, by which all the steel for the Forth Bridge was produced, were Frederick Siemens in England and Pierre and Emile Martin in

Fig. 5.15. Men working on junction of Queensferry north-west leg and top girder of cantilever: note safety-conscious workmen in background(!) and temporary bolted connections (June 1888)

France; the commercially vital discovery of how to use phosphoric iron ores was made by S. G. Thomas and his cousin Percy Gilchrist in 1875. No doubt because of the early unreliability of Bessemer steel, the Board of Trade prohibited the use of steel in bridges in Britain until 1877—the contract for the steelwork of the Forth Bridge was let only 5 years later. The greater part of the steel for the cantilever spans, a total of 38 000 tons, was supplied by the Steel Company of Scotland; the Landore Works in South Wales supplied 12 000 tons; and Dalzell's Iron and Steel Works at Motherwell near Glasgow supplied the remaining 8000 tons. The Clyde Rivet Company, Glasgow, supplied about 4200 tons of rivets.

Fig. 5.16. (below) Navvy on the tramp, 1855

Fig. 5.17. (below right) Rock excavation on north approach viaduct: only man-power and horse-power in evidence (April 1888)

The contractors

The men who put their signatures to the tender dated 25 October 1882 for the construction of the 'Viaduct across the Forth' for the sum of £1 600 000 were 'Falkiner & Tancred, William Arrol, and Joseph Phillips' (Figs 5.9 and 5.10). In most accounts of the building of the Forth Bridge it is Arrol alone who is given the credit, and it is hardly necessary here to retell the story of his humble birth

in 1839, his struggles to find work, his enlistment in the Renfrewshire Rifles for 5 years, his employment as foreman at a starting wage of £2 per week in Laidlaw's Engineering Works in Glasgow, and his early business venture as boiler and girder maker in 1868 which very nearly collapsed when its first customer became insolvent.

Arrol's firm survived the crisis, and in 1875 gained the contracts for the Clyde viaduct at Bothwell and the Caledonian Railway bridge over the Clyde at the Broomielaw in Glasgow. At this time also he developed his hydraulic riveter which at a stroke halved the cost and greatly improved the quality of what had previously been done by hand.

Later, Arrol was awarded the contract to build Bouch's suspension bridge across the Forth at Queensferry, and preparatory work had begun when the failure of the first Tay Bridge in December 1879 caused the contract to be abandoned. For reasons not very clear in any of the sources I have been able to consult, when Fowler and Baker's design for the Forth Bridge was approved in 1882 they asked Joseph Phillips to estimate for the construction of the bridge, 'doubtless on account of his expert knowledge of large bridges', as his obituarist puts it.[12]

The contract was subsequently awarded to Phillips, his partners Sir Thomas Tancred and Travers H. Falkiner, and William Arrol, jointly as Tancred, Arrol and Co. As resident partner at South Queensferry for the contractors, Phillips bore the onerous responsibility for general management of the whole contract. Tancred, on the other hand, seems to have had very little to do with the actual work on the bridge, although 'On 6th June 1883 a ceremony was held just to the east of the church at North Queensferry, when Sir Thomas Tancred laid the first granite block with full masonic honours.'[13]

In fact, by 1886 Tancred's partnership with Falkiner had been dissolved. He thereafter carried out large contracts in Asia Minor and according to Ref. 1 was engaged in 1890 in constructing a railway across the isthmus of Tehuantepec in Mexico. Travers Falkiner was responsible for the railway connections from the bridge to the main lines at Dalmeny and Inverkeithing.

Other engineers working with Tancred, Arrol & Company included Andrew Biggart, in charge of the drawing offices, shops and yards, who published a number of important papers on the Forth Bridge and Arrol's Tay Bridge; William Gray, in charge of all excavation and masonry work; Ernest Moir, who was later (as Sir Ernest Moir) for some years the right-hand man of Lord Cowdray; Louis Neville, engineer on the approach railways; and Wilhelm Westhofen, engineer of the works on Inchgarvie and author of the definitive account of the Forth Bridge that appeared in *Engineering* on 28 February 1890.

An essential part in the construction of the bridge was played by Monsieur L. Coiseau, the subcontractor for the sinking of the caissons. As engineer-in-chief with the firm of Hersent & Couvreux he had been engaged for several years previously on the construction of the great quays and harbour walls and docks at Antwerp, also under compressed air, and his experience of this type of work was of great value.

The men of skill

Many of the tasks involved in the construction of the Forth Bridge required a high degree of skill and experience in the men who performed them, none more so than those of the divers (Fig. 5.11) who assisted in the taking of soundings and subsequently in the job of making the caissons watertight. Work in the caissons was of a similarly demanding nature, and although Coiseau brought with him a number of his own key men, Westhofen was at pains to stress that British workmen were equally capable of standing up to the pressures used. Conversely, the continental workers were affected just as much by 'the morning after the night before' as the natives!

In the building of the piers supporting the steel superstructure and the piers of the approach viaducts, granite facings and rubble hearting were used. Especially on the approach viaducts, where the whole of the steelwork was erected near ground level (Fig. 5.12) then raised all in one while the piers were built course by course underneath (Fig. 5.13), the skill and attention to detail required of the masons was obviously of a very high order.

By far the greatest part of the bridge is the steel superstructure—here a variety of skills were required, ranging from the preparation of the steel sections in the machine-shop, involving cutting, bending, planing, drilling etc. through the preliminary bolting-up in the yard (Fig. 5.14) and in situ (Fig. 5.15) to the final alignment and riveting. The men engaged in such work had to be suitably experienced: many of them would have worked previously on other Arrol bridge contracts, or in the shipyards in Glasgow and elsewhere.

As much of the work as could reasonably be so organized was done on piecework rates. Westhofen records that the hand-riveters worked in gangs of four, i.e. two riveters, one holder-up and one rivet-heater, generally a boy. These boys were not unaware of the vital part they played, and managed to negotiate a fixed weekly minimum wage of 20 to 24 shillings. The gang as a whole were paid an agreed sum per hundred rivets satisfactorily completed.

The men of muscle

'Taking them as a whole, it must be freely acknowledged that the workmen employed upon the bridge have not, to any material extent, added to the troubles and anxieties attendant upon such a work. Black sheep are found everywhere, and of the doings of such a tolerably lively account might easily be presented. Many of them—hundreds of them—were mere birds of passage, who arrived on the tramp, worked for a week or two, and passed on again to other parts, bringing a pair of hands with them and taking them away again, and having in the mean time made extremely little use of them except for the purpose of lifting the Saturday pay packet and wiping their mouths at the pothouse: many others also, who, too clean-shaven and too closely-cropped as to hair, vainly tried to deceive anyone as to the character of the hotel they were last staying at, or to invent a plausible account of the big job which they had just left completed.'

'But apart from these, it is no exaggeration to say that no one need desire

Fig. 5.18. One man and his shovel: 'Alone I done it!' (November 1888)

to have to do with a more civil or well-behaved lot of men, always ready to oblige, always ready to go where they were told to go, cheerfully obeying orders to change from one place to another, and, above all things, ready to help others in misfortune, not with advice but with hands and purses. Nor was there any difference in that respect on account of nationality: Scotch, English, and Irish were about equally represented as to numbers and though the latter furnished very few skilled hands, they were mostly very hard workers and very conscientious and reliable men.'

So wrote Wilhelm Westhofen, and in these two paragraphs he paints a colourful picture of 'the workmen', not only in what he says about them but even more, perhaps, in what he doesn't say! Other authors, notably Coleman[14] and Handley,[15] have told the story of the navvies (Fig. 5.16), who got their name from working on the early navigations and canals, then from about 1835 laboured in their thousands to build Britain's network of railways.

The work involved earth moving, rock cutting (Fig. 5.17) and tunnelling, bridge building and track laying, using only man power (Fig. 5.18) and horse power, often in remote and inhospitable parts of the country, living hard and rough and earning (in the first half of the nineteenth century) 3 d an hour, 15 shillings for a basic week of 60 hours. On many jobs unscrupulous contractors paid their navvies monthly instead of weekly, with the result that the majority of them, congenitally improvident, would be forced to seek a 'sub' at an exorbitant rate of interest by the middle of the month. Then of course, when pay-day finally came round, the subs were deducted with interest and they went on a wild drinking spree with what they had left, losing two or three more working days recovering from the after-effects.

The advance of an army of navvies into a previously peaceful and (relatively) law-abiding country district was something to be feared and resisted, and many a pitched battle was fought with the local inhabitants until the two sides could be separated by the intervention of the police, whose numbers were usually increased while the work was in progress; on not a few occasions the local magistrate had to read the Riot Act and call up the militia to restore order.

As in so many other ways, the construction of the Forth Bridge heralded a time of rapid change in the methods of building both railways and bridges, and in the conditions of employment for the men working on them. Wages in the second half of the nineteenth century had increased to 4 d or 4½ d an hour for the labourers or navvies, known to the locals as the 'briggers'. Skilled men such as platers could earn 7 d or 8 d an hour, and some of the best and hardest working riveters could make £3 in a good week, though even for them the average was nearer £2.

Some of the biggest changes resulted from the growing use of steam-powered plant of all kinds, including locomotives large and small; paddle-steamers and tugs; cranes and winches; electric generators for the arc lighting;

Fig. 5.19. (facing page, top) Progress of erection, May 1889

Fig. 5.20. (facing page, bottom) 'Tin Town' (from an old photo): said to have been located on the north side of the Forth for workers on either the Forth Bridge or Rosyth Dockyard (started in 1908)

Fig. 5.21. Houses at Rosshill Terrace

air compressors; high pressure water pumps for hydraulic rams, riveters and power tools; 'steam navvies' for excavation; and all manner of workshop tools and equipment. Many of the most useful items of plant and construction equipment used on the bridge were developed or adapted specially for the Forth Bridge contract by William Arrol, who had a particular talent in that direction.

Arrol was more concerned for the welfare of his workers than most other employers of that time, and he knew that no matter what general provisions were made for working conditions to be as safe as possible on the bridge at heights of up to 360 ft above the water (Fig. 5.19), accidents were bound to happen. Many of them were due to sheer carelessness or bravado, men and boys habitually 'walking the plank' or trusting themselves to ropes and ladders not properly secured. Special gangs of men were employed to clear

Fig. 5.22. Bridge House

up the litter of wood and metal that constantly gathered on the working platforms, nets were suspended wherever possible to protect those working at lower levels, and rescue boats were stationed beneath each cantilever, saving at least eight lives and recovering about 8000 caps and other items blown into the water.

In spite of all the precautions, accidents did happen, and between July 1883 and the end of 1889 there were 57 deaths, about 100 serious injuries and more than 500 minor accidents requiring medical treatment. Westhofen makes the point (which could no doubt be echoed by the Health and Safety Executive today) that 'Fully three-fourths of all more serious accidents were due entirely to what may strictly be called preventible causes.'

On the other hand, there were some remarkable escapes. Baker himself told the story of one man who trusted himself at a great height to his grasp of a rope, but becoming numb with cold relaxed his grip and fell backwards 120 ft down into the water from which he was fished out little the worse. In another incident, Baker saw a hole one inch in diameter made in the 4 inch timber of a working platform by a spanner which had fallen about 300 ft, having taken off a man's cap in its descent without causing him a scratch; and he knew of another dropped spanner which entered a man's waistcoat and came out at his ankle, tearing open his clothing but not injuring him in any way.

In the summer of 1883 a Sick and Accident Club was started, membership of which was compulsory for all the contractors' employees, the subscription being one hour's pay per week to a maximum of 8 d. Medical treatment was available to the men and, to a limited extent, their families, and if they were unable to work weekly payments of 9 to 12 shillings could be made from the funds. Funerals were paid for within certain limits, and grants were made to widows, wives and children of men killed or permanently disabled at work. The contractors paid a sum of £200 annually into the club, and gave a good deal of other assistance.

The number of men employed on the bridge naturally varied as construction progressed, and was less in winter than in summer; the number rose to over 4000 in the summer of 1887, and to its highest level, 4600, the following year. Lodgings were available locally for only a small proportion, but Arrol was determined that there should be no 'living rough', and on both sides of the water erected tolerably comfortable hutted living quarters (Fig. 5.20) together with stores for the sale of food and clothing, and a canteen and reading rooms.

To these were added, according to Westhofen, 'sixteen houses substantially built in bricks for the accommodation of foremen and members of the staff, and about sixty tenements at Queensferry for leading hands and gangers.' The houses are now numbers 1 to 16 Rosshill Terrace, Dalmeny Station, some of them rendered over the brickwork but others still much as they must have looked more than a hundred years ago (Fig. 5.21). It is interesting to note that number 16 is occupied by a J. M. Telford!

The 60 tenements at Queensferry to which Westhofen refers must have been tenements in the old English sense of flats or dwellings, not *blocks* of flats as understood in Scotland. No trace of them now remains, but there is near the bridge a large house of rather English appearance which on the Ordnance plan of 1895 is called 'Forth Bridge House', and is now known simply as 'Bridge House' (Fig. 5.22). Although not mentioned by Westhofen, it is well-known locally that this house was built for the senior staff engaged on the construction of the Forth Bridge.

The populations of places near the bridge , as given in the census of 1881, were:

South Queensferry	1966
Winchburgh	115
Kirkliston	747
North Queensferry	360
Inverkeithing	2565

Fig. 5.23. 'Eric de Maré'
view of central pier

When work on the bridge was at its height, therefore, arrangements were made with the North British Railway to run special trains connecting the works with Edinburgh and Leith on the south side, and Inverkeithing and Dunfermline on the north side. On these workmens' trains purely nominal fares were charged, for example a weekly ticket to and from Edinburgh cost only 2 shillings. 'In the summer time', adds Westhofen, 'a steamboat service was also arranged between the South Queensferry Jetty and Leith, via the Firth of Forth, calling both ways on Inchgarvie, and so long as the weather was favourable, this was a most enjoyable, and certainly healthy trip for the tired workmen.'

Critics and champions

One of the earliest critics of the Forth Bridge was a man who might well have thought it advisable not to comment publicly on another major civil engineering project. Sir George Biddell Airy (1801–92), the Astronomer-Royal from 1835 to 1881, was a Fellow of the Royal Societies of London and Edinburgh, President several times of the Royal Astronomical Society, and a Member of the Institution of Civil Engineers, to whom in 1867 he presented a paper on long-span stiffened girder suspension bridges.

He was not a man to hold his tongue or put down his pen until he had had his say, and in his long life published eleven books and over 500 papers, articles and reports. When consulted by Bouch on the wind pressure for which his 1873 Forth suspension bridge should be designed, he suggested a figure of 10 lbs/ft^2. A few years later, quite unabashed, on seeing Fowler and Baker's cantilever design he wrote in an article that in his opinion a suspension bridge would be much better, and that 'we may reasonably expect the destruction of the Forth Bridge in a lighter gale than that which destroyed the Tay Bridge.'

At the opening ceremony of the Forth Bridge in 1890 Sir John Fowler (as he had just become) said: 'It is very curious to watch the manner of retreat of these prophets of failure when results prove they have been mistaken, and I could tell you some very curious stories. But on this day I feel I can afford to be magnanimous, and I shall say nothing ill-natured about any of them—not even the astronomers.'

William Morris (1834–96) has been described as a pivotal figure of his age: he made his mark as a poet, translator, novelist, painter, designer and writer. His ideal was 'simplicity of life begetting simplicity of taste'. Unadorned simplicity and directness in the expression of structural function lay at the heart of Baker's approach to design, and might have been expected to merit Morris's approval. But the Victorians were full of contradictions, and a few months before the Forth Bridge was opened Morris declared: 'There never will be an architecture in iron, every improvement in machinery being uglier, until we reach the supremest specimen of all ugliness—the Forth Bridge.'

This time Benjamin Baker gave the answer in an address to the Edinburgh Literary Institute.

'It is impossible for anyone to pronounce authoritatively on the beauty of an object without knowing its functions. The marble columns of the Parthenon are beautiful where they stand, but if we took one and bored a hole through its axis and used it as a funnel of an Atlantic liner, it would, to my mind, cease to be beautiful, but, of course, Mr Morris might think otherwise.'

One thing at least about the bridge was not in dispute—its colossal size meant that it could not be ignored; it dominated the landscape, and

Fig. 5.24. 'Euclid' view of geometry of bridge

demanded a response from all who saw it. The response of John Ruskin (1819–1900), stern critic of art and architecture, was unequivocal. He believed that the most beautiful things in the world are the most useless; peacocks and lilies, for instance. Having seen the bridge for the first time, he said he wished he had been born a blind fish in a Kentucky cave.

On the other hand, Alfred Waterhouse, RA (1830–1905), a noted neo-Gothic architect, wrote to Fowler:

'One feature especially delights me—the absence of all ornament. Any architectural detail borrowed from any style would have been out of place in such a work. As it is, the bridge is a style unto itself; the simple directness of purpose with which it does its work is splendid, and invests your vast monument with a kind of beauty of its own, differing though it certainly does from all the beautiful things I have ever seen.'

Only a few of the countless other opinions expressed during the Forth Bridge's hundred-year life can be recounted here. One of the most respected must be that of Eric de Maré, the outstanding photographer of architectural and engineering subjects, in his book '*Bridges of Britain*' (1954).

'When completed it staggered the world and it remains an extraordinarily impressive spectacle—a national symbol for Scotland . . . The design scorns all affectation; it has a difficult job to do and it does it with a simple, functional directness and a superb, unselfconscious confidence.' (Fig. 5.23).

The designer of the George Washington Bridge in New York, David B. Steinman, with Sara Watson wrote '*Bridges and their builders*' (1941), in which volume a whole chapter is devoted to the Firth of Forth Bridge:

'The natural setting is breath-taking in its beauty, but . . . also (in construction) unavoidably involved adverse and treacherous weather conditions. In such a setting the Forth Bridge looms like a giant dinosaur stretching itself out in the sun. Such a sight cannot be called beautiful or pleasing, but rather it is overpowering, awesome, colossal. The Forth Bridge seems to scorn beauty, even seems to revel in a certain awkward angularity, for it boasts of invincible strength, in which it glories with superb indifference and with insolent pride.'

Anthony Murray[16] remarks that the distinguished art critic and historian Sir Kenneth (later Lord) Clark elevated the Forth Bridge into the realms of High Art when he included a photograph of it on the back cover of his classic work '*Civilisation*' (1969). Interestingly, the front cover shows a detail from Raphael's fresco in the Vatican known as the 'School of Athens', which shows Euclid proving a geometrical theorem to an admiring group of young men. Euclid would certainly have been fascinated by the Forth Bridge, which so clearly demonstrates its derivation from his theorems (Fig. 5.24), even though (or perhaps because) in Lord Clark's words: '. . . it is an anachronism, a sort of prehistoric monster—a brontosaurus of technology'.

The last tribute that must be recorded here was paid to the bridge in 1985 when a plaque was unveiled on the pier facing the Edinburgh road near the Hawes Inn. The (British) Institution of Civil Engineers and the American Society of Civil Engineers combined to dedicate the Forth Bridge as an 'International Historic Civil Engineering Landmark'.

The Forth Bridge is indeed like few other man-made structures, one of the wonders of the modern world, a magnificent example of Victorian enterprise and engineering, a symbol of the men behind the bridge, and a memorial to the men who died in its creation.

Acknowledgements

My grateful thanks are due to Richard Packer of the Department of Civil Engineering, Imperial College of Science and Technology, for his excellent reproductions of the original Evelyn Carey progress photographs which make up the majority of my illustrations. The 'commemorative portrait group' (Fig. 5.1) was only recently discovered in the office of the legal firm who had been the solicitors for the Forth Bridge Railway Company; it was kindly made available by Douglas McBeth of the Forth Bridges Exhibition Centre. The illustration of the 'Navvy on the tramp, 1855' (Fig. 5.16) is from Ref. 14, by permission of Messrs Hutchinson, London. The original print of 'Tin Town' (Fig. 5.20) was made available by Old Scotland in Pictures, 107 Brunswick Street, Edinburgh.

References

1. Westhofen W. *The Forth Bridge*. Reprinted from *Engineering*, London, 28 February 1890.
2. Tolstoy I. *James Clerk Maxwell*. Canongate, Edinburgh, 1981.
3. Charlton T. M. *A history of theory of structures in the nineteenth century*. Cambridge University Press, 1982.
4. Channel D. F. *William John Macquorn Rankine*. Edinburgh University, 'Scotland's Cultural Heritage' series, 1986.
5. Birse R. M. *Engineering at Edinburgh University: a short history 1673–1983*. Edinburgh University, School of Engineering, 1983.
6. Mackay T. *The life of Sir John Fowler, Engineer*. John Murray, London, 1900.
7. Hammond R. *The Forth Bridge and its builders*. Eyre and Spottiswoode, London, 1964.
8. *Dictionary of National Biography*. Oxford University Press, 1885 *et seq*. (22+8 vols).

9. Baker B. Long Span Bridges. *Engineering*. London, 1867.
10. *Proc. Instn Civ. Engrs,* **119,** 399–400.
11. Derry T. K. and Williams T. *A short history of technology.* Clarendon Press, Oxford, 1960.
12. *Proc. Instn Civ. Engrs,* **164,** 417.
13. Douglas H. *Crossing the Forth.* Robert Hale, London, 1964.
14. Coleman T. *The railway navvies.* Hutchinson, London, 1965.
15. Handley J. E. *The Navvy in Scotland.* Cork University Press, Cork, Ireland, 1970.
16. Murray A. *The Forth Railway Bridge: a celebration.* Mainstream, Edinburgh, 1983.

Bibliography

Sir William Arrol & Company, *Bridges,* (For private circulation) *Engineering,* London, 1909.

Dickenson H. W. and Titley A. *Richard Trevithick: the engineer and the man.* Cambridge University Press, 1934.

Mackay S. *The Forth Bridge: a picture history.* Moubray House, Edinburgh, 1990.

Marshall J. *A biographical dictionary of railway engineers.* David and Charles, Newton Abbot, 1978.

Murray A. *The Forth Railway Bridge: a celebration.* Mainstream, Edinburgh, 1983.

Purvis Sir Robert. *Sir William Arrol: a memoir.* Blackwood, Edinburgh, 1913.

Thomas J. *The North British Railway (vols 1 and 2).* David and Charles, Newton Abbot, 1969 and 1975.

CHAPTER 6

Crossing the Forth in 2090

Professor E. Happold, *School of Architecture and Building Engineering, University of Bath*

Introduction

I have been asked to predict the future—a very dangerous game. Perhaps if one can remember the past, one can remember the future. In designing, one conceives of directions and opportunities, and then uses past experience— history, if you like—to determine how to react. It can certainly be stated that without 'assembling materials to sustain load', life could not exist. Although the first (and still the most efficient) structures evolved in nature, it is humankind that has deliberately made structures for its own purposes.

The continuation of this development is a difficult topic to examine, because structural engineers' problems are very broad. On the one hand they study science—how phenomena in nature are explained—while on the other they try to realise projects in a complex political and social world. Any prediction must therefore take account of future development in all its facets, including the development of structural engineering as a profession, or new methods and new relationships, what the products will be made of and what actions they will be subject to.

There has been steady growth in recent times in understanding of the science we need—climatic forces, materials characteristics, their behaviour in structures etc. However, such growth has always been either resisted or encouraged by the socio-economic environment of the time. Thought develops constantly; utilisation is dependent on what is seen as desirable. This will dictate the future.

The past

Before the 19th Century
Consider the past. In the classical world, basically a slave-owning society, there was little need to develop mechanical power or new structural materials. The apprentice was taught what would work by the craftsman master. Efficiency was of little interest.

Mediaeval society confirmed this tradition; the Church's view of life as a religious mystery inhibited enquiry. The non-conformism of the Renaissance overcame such superstitions, and a wave of scientific enquiry began.

Fig. 6.1. (above) The Eiffel Tower

Fig. 6.2. (above right) The Brooklyn Bridge

Studying nature and determining how it acts became a division of knowledge in its own right, and began to stimulate innovation. The invention of Savery's atmospheric pump and Thomas Newcomen's steam engine were products of these advances in understanding, leading to machines to drain mines and drive furnace bellows.

By the end of the 18th century, population pressures on the land and the broader availability of knowledge brought about an increased realisation of the creativity of more of the population. Cheap iron started to be produced in Coalbrookdale using coal, rather than wood, as fuel. This was the beginning of the era of using non-renewable resources—metals and fossil fuels. In 1779 the first iron bridge was erected at Coalbrookdale, and in 1801 the first full-sized steam locomotive was built by Trevithick at Camborne. The next century witnessed great engineers solving an amazing range of problems: at this point I must acknowledge that I am at this moment almost literally in the shadow of a great structural monument, in the centenary year of its opening. I refer, of course, to the Firth of Forth Railway Bridge. Like the Brooklyn Bridge and the Eiffel Tower, which have also recently attained 100 years, the design of the Forth Bridge was just extremely innovative—because of its scale and the environment in which it was built, it has become symbolic.

19th Century triumphs

The American architect, James Marston Fitch, cited the three great triumphs of the 19th century as 'the Eiffel Tower for its conquest of height, the Brooklyn Bridge for its conquest of span and the Crystal Palace for its conquest of space' (Figs 6.1–6.3). Two of these have come to represent their cities, if not their countries—the Crystal Palace, alas, is no more. At a deeper level than the visual they are expressions of enterprise, organisation and technical innovation. The Eiffel Tower represented a structural answer to wind forces, the Brooklyn Bridge introduced wire rope spinning as a means to carry tension, and the Crystal Palace developed prefabrication to provide economy and speed of construction.

So has it been with the Firth of Forth Bridge. It represents Scotland, but also much more. This is the basis of my look into the future.

The men who built the bridge are interesting. They came from many lands—of the contractors, Sir William Arrol was a Scot, Thomas Tancred an Irishman, Le Coiseau a Frenchman; there were also a New Zealander and a Japanese. But this was not important in those days; the bridge was for the North British Railway and Britain had the largest empire in the world.

The two men who really interest me, in terms of education, training and personality, were the two partners and chief designers, John Fowler and Benjamin Baker.

The engineers

John Fowler was born in 1817 near Sheffield. The Stockton and Darlington Railway Line was opened when he was 8 years old; the Liverpool and Manchester when he was 13. As he did not die until 1898, his experience spanned almost a century.

After education at a private school, Fowler, the son of a land surveyor, was apprenticed to Mr J. T. Leather, engineer of the Sheffield waterworks, who was also engaged in canal and dock works. He extended this early training in hydraulics to railways in assisting Mr Leather's opposition to Robert Stephenson's proposal to exclude Sheffield from the main line of the Midland

Fig. 6.3. The Crystal Palace

Fig. 6.4. *Fleet Street and
Ludgate Hill, London in
the 19th Century*

Fig. 6.5. Metropolitan Railway: dignitaries on trial trip, 24 May 1862

A TRIAL TRIP.

METROPOLITAN RAILWAY, EDGWARE ROAD STATION.

Railway. Further work on railways led him to seek wider experience, and on completion of his pupilage in 1837 he went to work for J. U. Rastrick, one of the great railway engineers of the day, becoming chief assistant in the preparation of drawings and contracts for several railways. He returned to Leather, and then became general manager and locomotive superintendent of the Stockton and Hartlepool Railway and the Clarence Railway.

Those were early days in a fast-growing field, with experimentation on a working scale. Young men of ability moved quickly from one responsibility to another. At the age of 26 Fowler set up on his own, designing, promoting Bills through Parliament and supervising the construction of railways. Through this period of railway mania, when fortunes were made and lost, he kept his head and advanced his reputation. The work expanded, and Fowler moved to London with a long list of projects. Though competent, none of these were outstandingly innovative until he took up the construction of the Metropolitan Railways—the world's first public underground railway system. People's hopes were very high; great relief was anticipated for the streets, yet the difficulties envisaged appeared insurmountable (Fig. 6.4). In 1853 the first Act was obtained, for Edgeware Road to Kings Cross. Many well-known engineers said that it could never be built, that if it was build it would never work, and that if it did work no-one would travel on it. John Fowler not only solved the problems, but provided the confidence to continue (Fig. 6.5). The enormously successful project was extended to the Circle Line, and so on. Even today, all over the world—in Hong Kong, Baghdad, Seoul, Singapore—underground systems are being constructed because they transport people so effectively in urban areas.

Fig. 6.6. (above) Fowler's
proposal for a channel
ferry.

Fig. 6.7. (above
right) The Tay Bridge
disaster

Fowler also considered the Channel crossing, though in this case his sense of the possible, and perhaps his experience of the difficulties of tunnel ventilation, led him to declare his belief that a tunnel was premature and to take a prominent part in 1872 in proposing a channel ferry at Dover (Fig. 6.6.) This proposal, extremely thoroughly worked out, seems more of the the early part of this century than of the last. Fowler's energy in this as in other enterprises was immense, his standing exceptional. His ability to simplify problems, his great common sense, is always evident.

For many years Fowler acted as advisor to the Government of Egypt, for which service he was knighted by the Queen in 1885; he was asked by the Government of Italy to resolve a dispute between itself and the great patriot Garibaldi. Though quite imperious as he grew older, and very exact in business affairs, Fowler was sociable, good natured, and interested in the success of others.

He was 63 when first consulted on the Forth Bridge. There had been several previous designs to cross the Forth. In 1805 a double tunnel was proposed; in 1818 an exceptionally shallow but now quite contemporary looking cable-stayed bridge almost exactly on the present site was proposed by a James Anderson of Edinburgh. Crossing was by ferry until an Act of Parliament was passed in 1865 for a design by Thomas Bouch; the Forth Bridge Railway Company was formed in 1873 to carry out a design by Bouch of a suspension bridge with two large spans of 1600 ft each. The capital for the bridge was subscribed by the four principal railway companies interested in the east coast traffic, a contract was signed and work actually started.

Thomas Bouch was a well known engineer of his time, the inventor of the roll on-roll off ferry and a designer of bridges which stood until after World War II. Unfortunately, he was the designer of the ill-fated Tay bridge which collapsed in 1879 (Fig. 6.7), and investigations into the cause of the disaster disclosed gross underestimations of loading and inadequacies of manufacture

Fig. 6.8. The Forth Bridge under construction

and inspection, which destroyed public confidence in his Forth Bridge design. Certainly the scale and proportion of the latter are rather frightening. The central towers (from which the main chains are suspended) were to have been 550 ft above high water; the rail level, comprised of two lines of rails 100 ft apart, would have been 150 ft above high water. The foundations of the central tower would have gone down to a depth of 110 ft below high water. However, I am told that it could have been built.

Sir John Fowler, who owned an estate at Braemore, never allowed his family to cross the Tay Bridge—one of its defects was that the piers were too narrow for stability.

Fig. 6.9. The Maracaibo Bridge

The Forth Bridge

On 18 February 1881, the four railway companies wrote to their consulting engineers—T. Harrison, W. H. Barlow and John Fowler, associated with Benjamin Baker, asking two questions: whether or not a railway bridge across the Forth was feasible, and if so, what would be the best design. Various possibilities were examined, calculations and cost estimates were made and discussed by the four, with the result that a cantilever type of bridge was chosen as offering the cheapest and best solution. This finding was reported on 4 May 1881, and its realisation entrusted to Mr Fowler and his partner Mr Baker.

John Fowler's career to that date could have been regarded as a contribution to the early history of the civil engineering profession—one only has to read about regular Tuesday evening dinner parties at his house at 2 Queen Square Place, London, attended by the younger Stephenson, Locke, Brunel, Bidder, Scott-Russell, Rendel and Hawkshaw to get the flavour. His partner Benjamin Baker was 20 years younger, and of entirely different personality and style. Science was seen as having taken over from experimental pursuit—as Baker said again and again of the Forth Bridge, 'The merit of the design, if any, will be found, not in the novelty of the principles underlying it, but in the resolute application of well tested mechanical laws

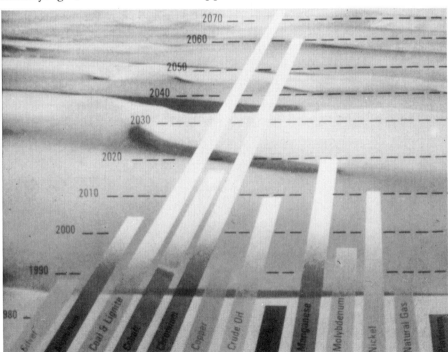

Fig. 6.10. Resources: 'the emptying storehouse'

and experimental results to the somewhat difficult problem offered by the construction of so large a bridge across so exposed an estuary as the Firth of Forth'.

Baker was much more the specialist of the two. His training started in the iron works of South Wales, where Trevithick's first Cornish pumping engines had been fabricated 100 years before. There he acquired practical experience in foundry, forge and manufacturing processes, and design of machinery and ironwork of all kinds, extending this experience into surveying, masonry and brickwork before joining John Fowler in 1861 at the age of 24. He became a partner in 1875.

Knighted at the opening of the Forth Bridge, Baker's relationship with Fowler was intensely close, strengthened perhaps by his never marrying. Fowler and he had complete control of the entire operation of building the bridge—a large staff was required, and control of the work lay mainly with Baker. His work record, by modern standards, is enormous. Perhaps we would most admire him for his repair and successful defence from demolition of Telford's Menai Suspension Bridge and Buildwas cast iron arched bridge.

Fowler and Baker could be typical partners today, one providing broad clear vision, the other detailed care and thoroughness. Each had great respect for the other. Qualification to be allowed to design structures takes far longer today, chartered status being achieved largely by input rather than output. While the image of the industry may not be as attractive in the next century as it was in 1890—after all, the top of the profession in those days made as much money as accountants do today—I suspect that the types and the range of abilities of engineers will still be the same.

Fig. 6.11. (below left) An efficient structure from nature

Fig. 6.12. (below) Human muscles show strain in response to an electrical impulse

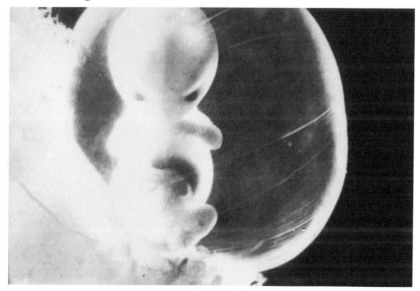

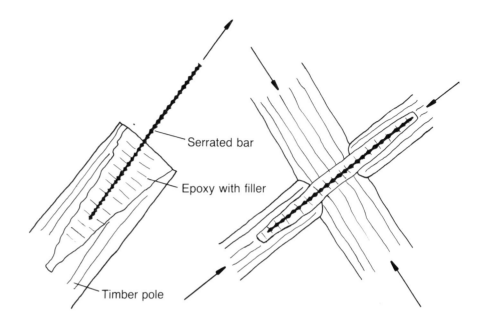

Serrated bar

Epoxy with filler

Timber pole

The biographies of the two designers clearly express a point of change. 1890 was almost the end of the period when the public was highly aware of the great civil engineers and their triumphs. Their influence on Britain, indeed on the world, was huge. Cheap iron and steel, the growth of railway and sea travel, the increased expectation of life due to public health engineering, water supply and sewage disposal—all of these had been developed by this very young profession.

The bridge was part of that turning point, partly because of its size, which is still very impressive. It is over 1½ miles long, and when built had the largest clear span in the world, comfortably exceeding that of the Brooklyn Bridge which in any case was designed only for horse-drawn road traffic. It was the second highest steel structure in the world, exceeded only by the Eiffel Tower (Gustave Eiffel attended the bridge's opening). It took 7 years to build, etc., etc.

The structural form was not new, but had not previously been used on such a scale. The method of fabrication, using large riveted tubes for the compression members, was not new either. Brunel had used similarly sized riveted tubes at Chepstow and Saltash 30 years before. It has been said that the Forth Bridge is overmassive in design, in reaction to the failure of the Tay Bridge.

Not only did Fowler and Baker take extreme care in defining the wind loads

Fig. 6.14. Experimental school made of wood

Fig. 6.15. Aerial view of experimental roof.

for the Forth Bridge, but Baker also carried out numerous pressure measurements as the bridge was constructed to confirm their assumptions, and operated extremely rigorous quality control—in this he must have been encouraged by Bouch's site huts, jetty and one foundation remaining as a memory of his passing. Failures leading to advances in knowledge have been a recurring feature in structural engineering. I remember, only some 10 years ago, struggling to determine reasonably accurate snow loadings for a 36 acre air-supported roof to cover the town centre of a mining community by the Athabasca River in Alberta. Considerable work had already been done, especially in North America and Eastern Europe, to categorise types of snow, their behaviour and effects; considerable effort had been expended to convert these into loadings useful to engineers. As far as Buro Happold is concerned, however, studying the recent failure of the Minneapolis Stadium air-supported roof has advanced our knowledge and understanding immensely. The need to apportion blame often generates more research work than an engineer can ever get finance for when initially designing—it also makes lawyers richer!

Yet perhaps the characteristic one most recognises in the designers is courage—not based on dreaming, as is one's impression of Bouch's design for the Firth of Forth, but on confidence in a team's thoroughness and competence, and in its ability to conceive a well-conditioned structure. Would we carry it out so clearly and so courageously now—and what of the future? We have a far greater understanding of structural behaviour and, since the invention of computers, much greater power to 'number-crunch'. Some believe that the use of computers by students as though they were 'black boxes' will inhibit true understanding of structures, but I do not share this view. The ability to carry out calculations much more quickly than in the past means that one can look at the implications of various actions faster. We can know more about what we are doing, and this is a help, not a hindrance. Computers are important in that they allow us to handle more data, but leaps forward are conceptual rather than mathematical.

Strong factors inhibit innovation and courage. The change in this country from a view of designers as professionals, who advise a client for a percentage fee, to competitive bidders for work is an inhibitor. If design means thinking out what to build before building '' because it is cheaper to do so, the cheapest design price will not necessarily the cheapest and most effective design. Combine this problem with the growing threat of litigation for real or imagined deficiencies in the product, and it is not surprising that some design firms make a great fuss about how simply they design yet appear to spend most of their time avoiding taxes and legal responsibility. I feel that engineering design from consultants has become more conservative and less innovative, and suspect that this trend will continue. Advances will tend to come from design and construct firms where the rewards of success are greater, and the rewards of failure cause company rather than personal liquidation.

Certainly, the Firth of Forth Bridge showed very clearly that one cannot separate design from construction. It is wonderfully illustrated in Westhofen's great book; it was in all the newspapers of the day (Fig. 6.8). Today in our firm we do not design unusual structures without simultaneously analysing the construction sequences—in fact, I doubt that we do any structures without a method statement and programme. The quality of management of construction delivers a product on time, at the lowest cost and the highest profit—safety is part of this, and will become more important. Some 57 died on the bridge; at the time this was blamed mainly on the work force! It would not be so easily accepted today—the care devoted to plant design and to the development of robotics will undoubtedly grow, leading to the question of whether or not every structure in 100 years' time will be carried out by design and construct firms. I doubt it. While savings in construction can be made by contractors being able to use their own

Fig. 6.16. Internal view of experimental roof

equipment as economically as possible, it is the finished product rather than the construction method that interests the client. Understanding this and designing to achieve it is not the same thing as construction management. The client needs a debate on the two objectives; this requires two firms.

Most interesting of all to a structural engineer, however, is the development in materials. The bridge was the first major structure in Britain to be made of mild steel. This material, of course, derived partly from the invention of Sir Henry Bessemer in 1855 of removing excess carbon from pig iron by blowing air through it, and partly from Robert Mushet's (another Scotsman) invention in 1856 of adding spiegeleisen, a form of iron and manganese, to the molten metal to remove sulphur impurities. Although the price of steel fell by more than a factor of ten, its use was resisted by many, including a committee of the Institution of Civil Engineers, because of its tendency to rust. Fowler and Baker resisted that advice; some 50 000 tons of mild steel was used in the bridge. As Sir Benjamin Baker said at the time—'as long as men painted it, so would it stand'.

This period was the start of the second part of the steel age. Britain led because it had extensive deposits of coal and of iron ore. Not until the Siemens–Martin open hearth system of making steel did it become easy to smelt basic ore. More easily mineable, therefore cheaper, basic ore deposits in Europe and America were then developed. That age is ending now.

The present
Baker was the precursor of the next generation. Large scale civil engineering work declined and was domesticated. Machine development became the next

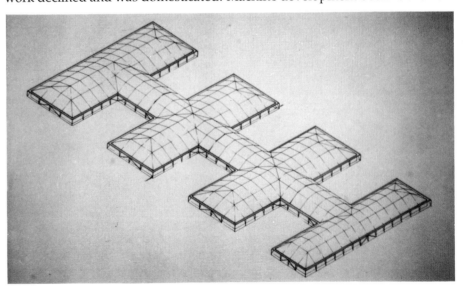

Fig. 6.17. Experimental foil roof with tendons

engineering frontier for communication (the telephone, the wireless, television), for human comfort (electricity, light, power) and for transport (cars, aeroplanes etc.).

Cheap fuel, cheap metals, the handbook and the code of practice have enabled simple, safe, easy structural design. Cost saving derived from mass production, a system which dictated a pace of work and grew out of the characteristics of metals. Fashion developed and price levels corresponded to appearance rather than function. Only in the aircraft industry was the efficiency of a structure of paramount importance, and the cost of failure death.

So, our approach to crossing the Forth would not differ greatly today, as is proved, I feel, by Ricardo Morandi's design for the Maracaibo Bridge (Fig. 6.9). Prestressed concrete replaces mild steel, but that is an obvious advance in terms of cost of maintenance.

The future

I believe that the big developments will be in materials, enabling us to continue to develop new types of structures. There are strong forces acting here. The price of fuel will rise, and we must reduce pollution. Structure will have to be determined on an energy basis, leading to big, albeit slow, changes. It is not the *amount* of energy used that is important, but rather to use it in a harmonious way (Fig. 6.10).

What will this mean for structures and structural engineers? It must mean a very different form of examination of the efficiency of materials—an examination of the 'costs' of production as well as construction and

Fig. 6.18. German castle with glass roof

maintenance. For example, the use of stone for domestic buildings may seem to require little energy, but the cost of cutting may be high. Its insulation value may not be great, the building may be expensive to use, and so on.

Most of all, these factors will challenge the use of metals. During the past 100 years structural engineers have tended to believe that metals, especially steel (even if used to reinforce concrete) are the true structural materials. It is easy to see why. They have high tensile and compressive strengths, they are homogeneous and easy to design in. They have straight stress-strain curves up to a point, and then forgive mistakes by redistributing load through ductility. But their structural efficiency in terms of load carried in proportion to weight is not high. Taking into account the energy costs of manufacture, a whole new set of conditions will apply.

We carry a lot of baggage from the past—pieces of knowledge which we have learnt to look at in a certain way. We usually conceive a structure from precedent or prejudice, and then use our numerical techniques to predict its performance. Methods are now being evolved (force density, structural loading coefficients etc.) to enable the production of an optimum structure from a definition of desired performance. I suspect that we will have to relearn quite fundamentally about materials and structures. And we will have to look at nature, because in nature a structure may not be the optimum one, but it will be efficient (Fig. 6.11). Inefficient structures do not survive.

There are now people working in this area—biologists, materials scientists and structural engineers. Liam Hudson said recently that it is in the areas of interface between disciplines that the action lies. It is where biologists and structural engineers meet that the formal and contained ways of thinking about materials are broken down, and one starts to think of structures based on biological models. The work of Jim Gordon and his friends at Reading University has made such a connection.

It is well known that carrying a force in tension requires less material than in compression (except over short distances) and considerably less than in bending. The cell is the basic form of structure in nature, maintained by a difference in pressure; it carries load by change of shape rather than increase in stress. Structure is an energy system which is potentially unstable chemically as well as physically.

Some colleagues and I have recently become interested in plant cell systems. Hogweed is an appropriate one to study, because it grows in one year. Initially the hogweed operates on a turgo (liquid pressure support) system. The advantages of this are that it is very well able to take shock loading, it is not brittle, and because of fibre orientation in the cell walls it is difficult to break, while the energy input to keep it up is constant but very small. But when it grows to a certain height it needs to stiffen, and then suddenly puts in a burst of energy to convert some of its cell matrix to lignin. This lignification renders it stiff (and brittle), but it needs no further energy for structural support.

Fig. 6.19. Lightweight Japanese house in Germany

This provides a lesson in structural design. The field of tensile structures has suffered from failures in the USA, but these have been caused by inadequate design work, probably the result of fee competition. An airhouse—covered by a membrane supported by a small positive air pressure—requires constant but small energy input. Active systems in structures will increase. What we must do is to get nature, not expensive fuel, to supply them, as in suspension bridges and airhouses.

In terms of continuous energy input, the tent is difficult to better. The structure of a person is composed of tension and compression members. What we have not yet achieved—but will—is the use of piezoelectric materials, well-known to designers of gramophone needles a long time ago, which show strain in response to an electrical impulse. The Indian ropetrick is another example—muscles do it, and so will our structures (Fig. 6.12).

The use of natural materials will increase. Wood is a fibrous composite whose stiffness per unit weight is as good as that of steel. Steel costs some 60 times as much as wood per ton. Wood is about a quarter as strong as mild steel, therefore its specific strength is about four times that of steel. The problem is rotting. Wood can be sealed, but if it is in contact with metal the seal will be broken by corrosion. Our practice has done a school for John Makepeace, the furniture designer, to examine such problems. The wet wood poles are treated like wire ropes—each 'tube' is joined together with epoxy, whose stiffness is amended to match that of wood by adding fibre (Figs 6.13 and 6.14). Like wood, the epoxy over time and in the presence of water moisture will stress relieve itself. The trick is to get a joint geometry which cannot have its capillaries closed by sandpapering and can accept lateral

Fig. 6.20. Linear motor train

expansion and contraction due to moisture changes. Over 90% of full strength is attained. This exercise continues—so will others.

Will structural engineering as a discipline distinct from the broader field of building engineering still exist? The problems certainly will, but I feel that separate disciplines will be less isolated. There is now more interest in broad problems because of a stronger sense of community in the construction industry as well as the world. One gets deeply interested in all the facets of a problem; in the physics of the whole structure.

The problem of our 36 acre roof for Athabasca (Figs 6.15 and 6.16) was that of light. People need something of the entire spectrum of daylight on their eyes each day, and Teflon coated fibreglass excludes part of the spectrum. We looked at foils—their performance is marvellous, but the problem is that of the balloon. A round hole, a pin prick, increases the stress around itself by a factor of three. In a homogeneous material, the crack will spread, as it did in this structure which is no longer standing. We need tendons so that the released strain energy will not be transmitted. So we layer—we are now developing a roof with foil pillows for a hospital in London, and very cheap it is too (Fig. 6.17). We are using the same idea for an all-glass roof over a castle in Germany (Fig. 6.18). I could continue on this theme. Our field of discovery is fascinating—I wish I were 40 years younger.

The Firth of Forth Bridge, quite consciously on the part of Fowler and Baker, was not obscured by decoration. It owed its shape to nothing more than the principles of structure that lay behind it and, unlike the contemporary Tower Bridge, did not try to be a French chateau or a Gothic cathedral. As Crystal Palace was attacked by Ruskin, so was the Forth Bridge by William

Morris, who claimed that there would never be an architecture in iron, with every improvement in machinery being uglier and uglier, and saw the Forth Bridge as the supreme specimen of all ugliness!

The Prince of Wales opened the bridge. What would his great grandson have said—'Little use of local stone, not in the vernacular'? Yet new structures develop new aesthetics. Regardless of what Prince Charles thinks, I believe houses and the like will have to become cheaper to build and run, with concomitant changes in appearance. There is a public prominence of visual values in the UK, but an actual importance of functional values (Fig. 6.19), which is why our discipline is so exciting. It is an art rooted in social responsibility.

In 100 years time I suppose the train will be powered by a linear motor, invented in Britain but developed in Germany, because it uses so little energy and produces no pollution (Fig. 6.20). The distance between the train and the track is critical, although very little deflection is acceptable and the bridge must be 'stiff'. The speed will not be as high as now, because the view of the Forth is so important and many of the users will be tourists.

All this signifies is that the shape of 100 years ago will be as valid 100 years into the future. I think we will still be preserving the old bridge—with robotic painting machines. Even if we build a new bridge, it will have the same basic form, a double cantilevered diagonally braced tubular structure. The material will probably be organic, but the idea will be the same. Fowler and Baker were pretty good.

Result of Scottish Schools' Forth Bridge Competition

The most outstanding entry in the Scottish Schools' Competition 'Crossing the Forth in 2090' was in the secondary schools' category, from the pupils of 1AF and 1BF of Kirkcaldy High School, entitled 'The Bridge'.

These competitors envisaged a three-span bridge across the river, each span being half a mile in length. Their entry included a model of one span as shown here. The travelway of the bridge would consist of a group of four tubes bound together, in cross-section like a symmetrical four-leaf clover. The top and bottom tubes would take road vehicles, and the middle pair tube trains propelled by electromagnets. Also incorporated into the structure would be houses, shopping malls, hotels, restaurants and electricity generating stations. The travelway tubes would be supported by cables suspended from two tubular arches meeting at mid-span but splayed out at their ends to provide stability.

In formulating the design many aspects were considered. The structure must be kept simple to avoid high maintenance costs. It should be light and strong. Because of strong winds the structure would have to be aerodynamic. Provision would be made against corrosion and temperature effects. The variety and operational requirements of the crossing traffic would be a major consideration.

The pupils conducted simple experiments on structural members of different cross-sectional type before they decided on the tube form and various arrangements of members were tested before the tubular arch was chosen. In engineering terms their entry was basically excellent. Their proposal bears an uncanny resemblance to Santiago Calatrava's design for a new crossing of the Thames that was featured in *The Times* on 4 July 1990.

At Professor Happold's prize-giving on 3 April 1990 the video supporting the entry was shown to the audience and received with acclamation.

The other prizewinners were as follows.

- Best primary school—Riverside Primary, Stirling.
- Equal second primary schools—Fair Isle Primary, Kirkcaldy; Echline Primary, South Queensferry.

- Age 12–14 joint prizewinners—Kenneth Rochford and Evan Walker, McLaren High School, Callander.
- Age 10–12—Andrew Poppa, Echline Primary, South Queensferry.
- Age 9 and under—Gillian Birrell, Galside Primary, Dumfries.
- Special prize—Mark Hadjucki (6), Edinburgh Academy.

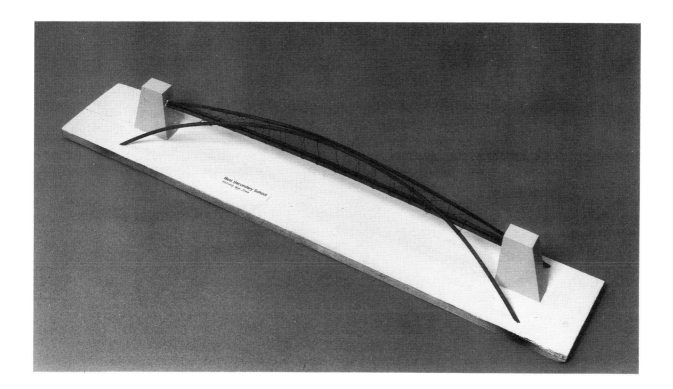

Index

Aberdeen, Lord and Lady, 79
Agricola, Georg (Bauer) (1490–1555), 8, 12
Airy, Sir George Biddell (1801–92), 138
Aitken, George, 110, 111
American Society of Civil Engineers, 94, 141
Anderson, James (c.1790–1861), 20, 42, 111, 148
Arrol, Sir William (1839–1913), 32, 44, 46, 65, 68–70, 77, 83, 90, 109–111, 120–121, 128–129, 134, 145
Athabasca, Alberta—air-supported roof, 154
Baird, Hugh (1770–1827), 3
Baker, Sir Benjamin (1840–1907), 43, 47, 49–64, 77, 90, 110–111, 120–123, 138, 150–152, 154, 156, 160–161
Bakewell, William N. (1845–1913), 110–111
Balbirnie, Samuel, 110–111
Bald, Robert (c.1778–1861), 14
Banffshire Railway, 123
Barlow, Peter William (1809–85), 118
Barlow, William H. (1812–1902), 32, 42, 44, 45, 118
Bateman, John F. (1810–89), 26
Bell Rock Lighthouse, 1811, 4
Bessemer, Sir Henry (1813–98), 127, 156
Bidder, George P., 'The Calculating Boy' (1806–78), 150
Biggart, Andrew S., 110–111, 129
Blackburn, James, 110–111
Blyth, Benjamin Hall (1819–66), 123
Bo'ness, coal pit, 13

Board of Trade, 41, 44, 47, 56, 67, 72, 90, 125–126, 128
Bouch, Sir Thomas (1822–80), 24–32, 36, 38, 40–43, 67, 111, 115, 123
Bourke, Walter S., 110–111
Brick, 32, 92, 151
Bridge
Alloa, proposed cast-iron, 1809, 4
Anderson's proposed chain, 1818, 18, 20, 22–24, 42, 111, 148
Bouch's proposed Forth suspension, 1871–80, 32, 41–48, 52, 123, 129, 154
Bouch's proposed viaduct at Charlestown, 1862–6, 26–32, 148
Bouch's Redheugh viaduct, Newcastle upon Tyne, 1871, 44, 51–52, 123
Bouch's Tay, 1878–9, 31–32, 36, 38, 40, 41, 44, 49, 55, 67, 71, 123
Britannia tubular, 1850, 27, 42
Brooklyn, 1883, 144–145, 152
Brunel's at Chepstow, 1852, 152
Buildwas, cast iron arch, 1796, 151
Cincinnati Southern Railway, Kentucky River, 1876, 47–48, 52
Clifton suspension, 1860, 118
Clyde viaduct, Bothwell, 1848, 69, 129
Coldstream, 1762–7, 2
Connel Ferry cantilever, Oban, 1903, 52, 55, 64

Bridge, continued
Eads' over the Mississippi, 1874, 126
Forth—see Forth Bridge
'Gerber girder' at Hassfort, 1867, 52
Landsdowne cantilever, India, 1888, 64
Maracaibo, 1957, 149, 157
Musselburgh, 1806, 4
Niagara cantilever, 1883, 50, 52
Perth, 1766–71, 2
Quebec cantilever, 1907, 65
Quebec cantilever, 1917, 52, 54, 65
Roebling's Niagara suspension, 1855, 118
Saltash, 1859, 27, 152
Schneider's Niagara cantilever, 1883, 52
Tay, rebuilding of, 1882–7, 56, 67, 69
Telford's Menai, 1826, 24, 42, 151
Torksey girder, 1850, 51
Tower, London, 1894, 160
Bridge House, South Queensferry, 136
Bridges
Caledonian Railway, River Clyde, Glasgow; 1876–8, 1899–1905, 69, 129
cast iron, 24, 144, 151
developments 1740–1817, 19–20
general design parameters, 38–40
influence lines, 61
long-span, Baker's study of, 120
masonry, 2
Severn, proposed in 1864

Bridges, continued
and 1871, 51
steel, 32, 41–48, 52
temperature effects, 44
wrought iron, 18–24, 26–32, 36, 38, 40–41, 44, 49, 51–52, 55, 69, 129
railway, developments 1830–50, 22, 24
Brown, Captain Sir Samuel (1774–1852), 19, 23–24
Bruce, Sir George of Carnock, 10, 12
Brunel, Isambard K. (1806–59), 27, 118, 150
Brunton, Spencer (Forth Bridge Railway Company), 110–111, 115
Buro Happold, 154
Cadell, Henry M. (1860–1934), 14–15
Calatrava, Santiago—proposed Thames bridge, 1990, 162
Caledonian Railway Company, 29, 113–114
Campbell, Duncan, 110–111
Carey, Evelyn (1858–1932), 109, 110–111, 124
Carron Ironworks, 2
Cement and concrete, 9, 75, 77, 92
Chalmers, Alex, 110–111
Chamberlain, Joseph (1836–1914), 67
Chapman, William (1749–1832), 16
Clark, Sir Kenneth (Lord Clark), 140–141
Clyde Rivet Company, Glasgow, 128
Coiseau, Monsieur L., 79, 129–130

'Columba' steam-ship, 1878, 56

Colville of Culross, Lord (1818–1903) (Great Northern Railway Company), 110–111, 115

Competition, Scottish Schools' — Crossing the Forth in 2090, 162–163

Cooper, Frederick E., 110–111, 124

Cooper, Theodore (1839–1919), 65

Cort, Henry (1740–1800), 19

Craig and Rose, paint manufacturers, 95

Crystal Palace, 1851, 144–145, 160

Culross, coal pits, 10–13

'Dalswinton' paddle steam-boat, 6

Dalzell's Iron and Steel Works. Motherwell, 128

De Maré, Eric (born 1910), 140

Dent, John Dent (1826–95) (North-Eastern Railway Company), 110–111, 115

Dodd, Ralph (c.1756-1822), 15-16

Dover — Channel ferry proposal, 1872, 148

Dowling, Charles, 27

Edinburgh and Glasgow Railway Company, 113, 115

Edinburgh, Perth and Dundee Railway Company, 111, 115

Eiffel Tower, 1889, 144, 152

Einstein, Albert (1879–1955), 116

Elgin and Kincardine, Earl of (1849–1917) (North British Railway Company), 110–111, 115

Energy basis for future structures, 157

Engineering design, nature of, 36

Engineering education, 10, 118

Epoxy joining of wooden structural members, 152, 159

Fairbairn, Sir William (1789–1874), 24

Falkiner, Travers H. (1829–

79), 68, 109, 129

Ferry
Fife and Midlothian, 6
Queensferry, 1–6, 9
rail — Granton to Burntisland, 9, 24, 26, 115
rail — Tayport to Broughty Ferry, 115

Fitzmaurice, Sir Maurice (1861–1924), 110–111

Foil pillow roof, 160

Forfeited Estates Commissioners, 1772–7, 1, 3

Forth and Clyde Canal, 1768, 1

Forth Bridge
Commemorative Portrait Group, 110–111
contract, 68–69
critics and champions, 138–141
deflection under load, 62, 90, 161
design, 56–64, 123–124, 152
design criteria, 49–51, 54, 56, 60, 62
erection of steelwork, 59, 85–90, 130, 133–134
fabrication, 59, 82–85, 124–125
foundations and piers, 74–82, 130
Fowler and Baker's proposals, 1881, 47
International Historic Civil Engineering Landmark, 94, 141
key dates in construction, 72–73
materials and stresses, 56
opening ceremony, 4 March 1890, 90, 161
Resident Engineers, 124
site preparation and setting out, 74–75
structural concept, 51–56, 118, 120
temperature effects, 61
the future, 157–161
theodolites, Cooke & Sons, 74
wind pressure, 54, 56, 60, 62
workers' conditions and wages; accidents, 86, 89–90, 130–137, 155

Forth Bridge House—see Bridge House

Forth Bridge maintenance
approach spans, 94–96, 161
cantilevers, 96–101, 161
cost, 105
internal viaduct, 102
masonry piers, 91–92, 94
staff, 105–107
suspended spans, 101–102, 161
track, 102–105

Forth Bridge Railway Company, 109, 115, 118

Fowler and Baker, consultants—see Fowler, Sir John

Fowler, Sir John (1817–98), 43, 47, 49–52, 55–56, 60, 90, 110–111, 118–124, 138, 145–152, 156, 160–161

Geology — Forth valley, 15

Gilchrist, Percy C. (1851–1935), 128

Glasgow, Hamilton and Bothwell Railway — bridges, 69

Glass roof over German castle, 160

Gordon, James E., Reading University, 158

Gordon, Lewis D. B. (1815-76), 118

Grainger, Thomas (1794–1852), 26

Gray, William, 110–111, 129

Great North Road Trustees, 4

Great Northern Railway Company, 115

Grieve, John, mining engineer, 13, 111

Harbour
Berwick, 1807, 4
Burntisland, 4, 9
Charlestown, 4
Granton, 9
Leith, 1804, 4
Newhaven, 1810, 4, 6
Perth, 1807, 4
South Queensferry, 1710, 1817, 1, 3
St Andrews, 1808, 4

Harris, David, 110–111

Harrison, Thomas E. (1808–88), 49, 118–119, 150

Hawkshaw, Sir John (1811–91), 118, 150

Health and Safety at Work Act, 1974, 96–97

Heygate, William U. (1825–1902) (Midland Railway Company), 110–111, 115

Hindlip, Lord (1842-97) (Great Northern Railway Company),110–111, 115

Hodgkinson, Eaton (1789-1861), 24

Hodgson, Richard (Chairman, North British Railway Company, c.1850–1866), 111, 114–115

'Holbein Straddle', 55–56, 61, 64

Hopetoun House, 13

Hudson, George, 'The Railway King' (1800–71), 114

Hudson, Liam (born 1933), 158

Hunter, Adam, 110–111

Hutchinson, Major-General Charles S. (1826–1912), 67, 72, 125–126

Hutton, Charles (1737–1823), 17

Hydraulic equipment, 26–27, 69, 75, 79, 85–86, 129, 134

Institution of Civil Engineers, 10, 94, 118, 119–120, 123, 141, 156

Iron
cast, 9, 10, 22, 24, 29, 41, 71
wrought, 9, 19–20, 22–24, 27

Jardine, James (1776–1858), 9, 20

Jessop, William (1745–1814), 17

Kelly, William (1811–88), 126–127

'Kippendavie'—see Stirling, John, of Kippendavie

Knowles, Arthur J., 110–111

Laidlaw's Engineering Works, Glasgow, 68, 129

Landore Steel Works, South Wales, 128

Learmonth, John (Chairman, Edinburgh and Glasgow Railway Company), 113–114

Leather, J. Towlerton (1804–85), 145

'Leviathan', ferry boat, 24

Lilliquist, Rudolph, 110–111

Linear motor rail systems, 161

Locke, Joseph (1805-60), 150

London — Fleet Street and Ludgate Hill c.1850, 146
Main, T. 110–111
Marindin, Major F. A., 126
Mavor, Alfred E., 110–111
Maxwell, James Clerk (1831–79), 59, 116–117
Meik, Patrick Walter (1851–1910), 110–111, 124
Metropolitan Railway (London Underground), 1853–65, 119, 147
Middleton, Reginald E. (1844–1925), 74, 110–111, 124
Midland Railway Company, 115
Millar, James (1762–1827), 14
Millar, William White, 110–111
Mining, undersea developments, 1575–1805, 10–13
Minneapolis Stadium — air-supported roof, 154
Moir, Sir Ernest W. (1862–1933), 110–111, 129
Morandi, Ricardo (born 1902), 52, 157
Morris, William (1834–96), 138, 160–161
Mushet, Robert F. (1811–91), 127, 156
Napier, Robert and Company, 24
Nasmyth, James (1808–90), 55
Neville, Louis, 110–111, 129
Newcomen, Thomas (1663–1729), 144
Noble, John (1828–96) (Midland Railway Company), 110–111
North British Railway Company, 30, 32, 111, 113–115, 120
North-Eastern Railway Company, 115, 119
Oakley, Sir Henry (1823–1912) (Great Northern Railway Company), 110–111
Phillips, Joseph (1828–1905), 68, 110–111, 129
Pier — Trinity Chain, 21
Piers — Queensferry, 2–6, 9, 32

Pole, William (1814–1900), 32, 44–45
Portraits, Forth Bridge Commemorative Group, 110–111
Preston, Sir Robert (1740–1834), 13
'Queen Margaret' paddle steam-boat, 6
Queensferry Passage—see Ferry, Queensferry
Railway — proposed Berwick to Kelso, 1808, 4
Railway Heritage Trust, 94
Rankine, William J. M. (1820–72), 117–118
Rastrick, John U. (1780–1856), 147
Rendel, A. M., engineer, 64
Rendel, James M. (1799–1856), 150
Rennie, John (1761–1821), 4–6, 16
Renton, James H. (1822–95) (Forth Bridge Railway Company), 110–111, 115
Ridley, Sir Matthew W. (1842–1904) (North-Eastern Railway Company), 110–111, 115
Roebling, John A. (1806–69), 27, 32, 38, 42, 118
Roman 'bridge of boats', 15, 19
Rosyth, proposed development at, 1806, 13
Royal Burghs of Scotland, 3
Ruskin, John (1819–1900), 140, 160
Russell, John Scott (1808–82), 150
Savery, Thomas (c.1650–1715), 144
Schluter, Axel, 110–111
Schneider, C. C., American engineer, 52
Scott, Thomas, 110–111
Scottish North Eastern Railway, 29
Siemens–Martin open-hearth steel, 127–128, 156
Smeaton, John (1724–92), 1–4, 7, 12, 19
Smith, C. Slater, American engineer, 52

St Pancras Station roof, 1868, 118
Steam engines and pumps, 9, 13, 16, 26, 74–75, 144, 151
Steel and steelmakers, 24, 41, 43, 50–51, 56, 63, 71–72, 88, 126–128, 152, 156, 159
Steel Company of Scotland, 128
Steinman, David B. (1886–1960), 140
Stephenson, George Robert (1819–1905), 27
Stephenson, Robert (1803–59), 24, 27, 42, 119, 145, 150
Stevenson, Robert (1772–1850), 6–7
Stewart, Allan D. (1831–94), 47, 59–60, 110–111, 123–124
Stirling, John, of Kippendavie (1811–82) (North British Railway Company), 111, 115
Strength of materials and structural theory, 9–10, 19–20, 23–24, 43, 56–62, 64–65, 116–117, 150, 156, 158–160
Symonds, A. J., 110–111
Tait, Peter G. (1831–1901), 116
Tancred, Arrol and Company — see Arrol, Sir William
Tancred, Sir Thomas (1840–1910), 68, 70, 109, 128–129, 145
Taylor, James (1753–1825), 13–14, 111
Taylor, John, 'The Water Poet' (1580–1653), 10–11
Teflon-coated fibreglass, 160
Telford, Thomas (1757–1834), 6–7, 9, 19, 23–24
Tensile structures, present and future, 157–160
Thomas, Sidney G. (1850–85), 128
Thompson, Sir Matthew W. (1820–91) (Midland Railway Company) 110–111, 115
Thornton, Robert, railway engineer, 27
Timber, 7–9, 23, 29–30, 94, 102–104, 159

Tin Town', navvies' huts, c. 1900, 132
Tone, John F. (1822–81), 27
Transport, nineteenth century progress in, 113
Tredgold, Thomas (1788–1829), 10
Trevithick, Richard (1771–1833), 16, 111, 144
Trustees for the Improvement of Fisheries and Manufactures, 3
Tuit, James E. (1860–1906), 110–111
Tunnel projects, pre-1807, 10–17
Tweeddale, Marquis of (1826–1911) (North British Railway Company) 110–111, 115
University of Cambridge, 116, 123
University of Edinburgh, 116, 117–118
University of Glasgow, 118
Vazie, Robert, 'The Mole', 15
Vazie, William, tunneller, 13, 15, 111
Walker, John (1828/9–91) (North British Railway Company), 110–111
Watanabe, Kaichi, Japanese engineer, 124
Waterhouse, Alfred, RA (1830–1905), 140
'Waverley' line, Edinburgh to Carlisle railway, 115
Webster, J. B., 110–111
Wembley Tower, 123
Westhofen, Wilhelm (1842–1925), 23, 42, 63, 89, 109, 110–111, 129, 155
Whitehaven, coal mine, 13
Wieland, George B. (Secretary of the North British and Forth Bridge Railway Companies), 110–111
Wind pressure, 30–31, 44, 47, 49, 54, 56, 60, 62, 138
Wood, E. Malcolm, 110–111
Wood, potential as a structural material, 159
Wylie, Jesse, site investigator, 29
York Station roof, 1877, 119